Insatiable
Appetites

Recent titles in
Contributions in Women's Studies

Women in the Resistance and in the Holocaust: The Voices of Eyewitnesses
Vera Laska, editor

Saints and Shrews: Women and Aging in American Popular Film
Karen M. Stoddard

Women of the English Renaissance and Reformation
Retha M. Warnicke

Face to Face: Fathers, Mothers, Masters, Monsters— Essays for a Nonsexist
Future
Meg McGavran Murray, editor

God's Handiwork: Images of Women in Early Germanic Literature
Richard J. Schrader

As Minority Becomes Majority: Federal Reaction to the Phenomenon of
Women in the Work Force, 1920-1963
Judith Sealander

Women in Colonial Spanish American Literature: Literary Images
Julie Greer Johnson

Divorce and Remarriage: Problems, Adaptations, and Adjustments
Stan L. Albrecht, Howard M. Bahr, and Kristen L. Goodman

Women and Death: Linkages in Western Thought and Literature
Beth Ann Bassein

Political Equality in a Democratic Society: Women in the United States
Mary Lou Kendrigan

Fantasy and Reconciliation: Contemporary Formulas of Women's Romance
Fiction
Kay Mussell

Three Who Dared: Prudence Crandall, Margaret Douglass, Myrtilla Miner—
Champions of Antebellum Black Education
Philip S. Foner and Josephine F. Pacheco

85200500

Insatiable Appetites

Twentieth-Century American Women's Bestsellers

Madonne M. Miner

CONTRIBUTIONS IN WOMEN'S STUDIES,
NUMBER 48

GREENWOOD PRESS
WESTPORT, CONNECTICUT • LONDON, ENGLAND

Library of Congress Cataloging in Publication Data

Miner, Madonne M.
  Insatiable appetites.

  (Contributions in women's studies, ISSN 0147-104X ;
no. 48)
  Bibliography: p.
  Includes index.
  1. American fiction—20th century—History and
criticism. 2. Women in literature. 3. American
fiction—Women authors—History and criticism.
4. Women—United States—Books and reading.
5. Popular literature—United States—History and
criticism. I. Title. II. Series.
PS374.W6M5 1984   813'.5'099287   83-18331
ISBN 0-313-23951-7 (lib. bdg.)

Library of Congress Catalog Card Number: 83-18331
ISBN: 0-313-23951-7
ISSN: 0147-104X

First published in 1984

Greenwood Press
A division of Congressional Information Service, Inc.
88 Post Road West
Westport, Connecticut 06881

Printed in the United States of America

10 9 8 7 6 5 4 3 2 1

Copyright Acknowledgments

Permission is gratefully acknowledged for the use of quo-
tations taken from:

Peyton Place by Grace Metalious, copyright © 1956 by
Grace Metalious. Reprinted by permission of Simon &
Schuster, a division of Gulf & Western Corporation.

Scruples by Judith Krantz. Copyright © 1978 by Steve
Krantz Productions. Used by permission of Crown Publishers, Inc.

To all my mothers . . .

Contents

Acknowledgments

In a sense, my Aunt Marsha is responsible for what follows. When I was twelve years old and quite capable of devouring novels by the dozens, she loaned me her well-worn copy of *Gone with the Wind*. I was transfixed and, at least temporarily, satiated. I now want to thank her for that loan, and to thank others who have made loans of a slightly different kind.

I am indebted to friends and colleagues—most especially Meg Kelley, Sarah Cliffe, Bruce Carey, Cathleen Carter, and Bob Torry—who have kept me alive and thinking; to Professors Mimi Goehlke and Mark Savin of the University of Minnesota, for their care and encouragement during my early graduate school years; to participants in the State University of New York at Buffalo Women's Writing Group, who read most of these chapters in rough draft and offered suggestions for revision; to Professors Claire Kahane, Leslie Fiedler, and John Dings of the State University of New York at Buffalo for their focused attention and insightful commentary; and to members of the University of Wyoming English Department.

And finally, I am most grateful to Professor Marcus Klein. Without him, the book could not have come into being.

Insatiable
Appetites

Introduction: "Guaranteed to Please the Female Reader"

> Of course it all began with my mother. . . . My love for her and my hate for her are so bafflingly intertwined that I can hardly see her. I never know who she is. She is me and I am she and we are all together. The umbilical cord which connects us has never been cut so it has sickened and rotted and turned black. The very intensity of our need has made us denounce each other. We want to eat each other up.
>
> —Erica Jong, *Fear of Flying*

On January 9, 1855, Nathaniel Hawthorne wrote a now-famous letter of complaint to his publisher, William D. Ticknor. According to the novelist, his works could not hope for success in the marketplace, since "America is now wholly given over to a d——d mob of scribbling women."[1] Recent scholarship not only corroborates Hawthorne's contention that women were muscling into the marketplace, but also provides us with a more complete account of this mob. In *Women's Fiction: A Guide to Novels by and about Women in America, 1820–1870,* for example, Nina Baym describes many of the white middle-class women who produced novels which sold in unprecedented numbers. Of course, description of the scribbling women provides us only with names of the ringleaders. Behind these women are the real mobsters: readers able to affect the marketplace by a show of their purchasing power. Although it is now impossible to procure precise demographic documentation of the audience which purchased seventy thousand copies of *Fern Leaves from Fanny's Portfolio*[2] or 2 million copies of novels by Mary Jane Holmes,[3] the amazing escalation of sales figures during the mid-nineteenth century leads literary historians to assume the presence of a new group of consumers within this audience: a group of women.[4] Prior to the boom in women's novels, white middle- and upper-class men both produced and purchased the majority of American texts. But in the early and middle decades of the nineteenth century, white middle-class women came to enjoy what formerly had been the exclusive prerogatives of their brothers: education, leisure, and perhaps, money for a few "luxury" purchases.[5] They moved into the literary marketplace, not only as writers, but also as readers, and readers with very specific demands.

The boom in women's texts indicates the beginning of a split between texts read by men and those read by women. Certainly, some men contributed to the popularity of Mrs. E.D.E.N. Southworth, Caroline Lee Hentz, Susan Warner, *et al.,* but evidence from the marketplace and from women writers themselves (who repeatedly address themselves to a female audience) suggests that for the most part men read texts by men, and women by women.[6] That male and female readers should have parted company when selecting texts comes as no surprise: they inhabited "separate spheres" on the basis of their sex.[7] These spheres defined possibilities not only of experience, but also of imagination. Thus, the woman forbidden by social convention from setting foot on a whaling ship might be inclined to reject the whaling tale in favor of the domestic novel, whose imaginary kitchen floors she literally trod upon every day.

Differences in men's and women's daily experiences contributed to the formation of a reading public split along sexual lines. But for a more complete understanding of gender-marked reading preferences, we first must ask about reading itself: why did these nineteenth-century men and women choose to spend their time reading? In its magnitude, the question appears impossible. Recent psychoanalytic theories of the reading process, however, suggest an answer. Nineteenth-century readers, just like readers today, derived pleasure from interacting with texts which "transform[ed] primitive childish fantasies into adult, civilized meanings."[8] While *consciously* engaging a text for "social, biographical, political, philosophical, moral, religious meaning" or for "escape, titillation, amusement," readers *unconsciously* engaged this text for the pleasurable transformation it allowed them to make of "primitive wishes and fears into significance and coherence."[9] This theory of reading suggests at least two corollary theories about textual preferences. First, since every individual adult reader will have experienced a range of childhood's wishes and fears, she/he may enjoy a range of texts, but certain texts will answer more closely to her/his own particular psychic structure. For example, the child who could not fully resolve conflicts of desire experienced during the oral phase may be unconsciously drawn, as an adult, to those texts which re-present and perhaps resolve oral conflicts. Even when confronted with a text not of her/his own choosing, the reader is " 'stimulated' only by those passages which he feels apply to himself. . . . Everything else leaves him cold."[10]

That individuals have different psychic experiences, different needs, and thus, different textual preferences, should be obvious. Equally obvious, but not introduced as an issue by Freud or critics from the reader response school, is a second corollary theory: since a fundamental differential factor in psychic experience is sex (developmental experiences are *not* the same for girls and boys), women, as a group, may choose different texts than those chosen by men to meet their different psychic needs. Interested primarily in male development, Freud never constructed an adequate model of female development nor did he consider fully how sexual differences in development might lead to differences in psychic strategies (here, strategies enacted in writing and reading). Feminist theorists correct Freud on both counts. Responding to Freud's first omission, Nancy Chodorow suggests that as early as the preoedipal phase, girls and boys partake of different developmental and relational experiences, primarily because in our culture (and in that of the nineteenth century as well) children of both sexes most often are raised by a parent of the female sex. Because of her own psychic experiences this female parent will "tend to treat infants of different sexes in different ways."[11] As articulated by Chodorow, this sex-specific treatment then produces sex-specific personality configurations (for example, women, nurtured by human beings of the same sex, may experience particular difficulties with individuation and separation).

Feminists with an interest in literary theory have begun to correct Freud's second omission. Originally concerned with differences in the writings of women and men, Annette Kolodny, Judith Gardiner, Nelly Furman, and others recently have extended their concern to include differences in reading and interpretation. All note the "crucial importance" of the *sex* of a reader or interpreter engaged in attributing "significance to formal signifiers."[12] This feature, previously ignored by critics Norman Holland, Harold Bloom, and Wolfgang Iser, may be a most important determinant in meaning construction. Combining the formulations of feminist psychoanalysts and literary theorists—both interested in the feminine personality and interpretation—we may deduce first: that women and men, treated differently as girls and boys, quite probably will have recourse in later life to different treatments, different texts; and second, that even when reading the same text, women and men quite probably will respond to, cathect with, and derive psychic satisfaction from different aspects of the text.

With this understanding of reading processes and preferences in mind, we may return to the mid-nineteenth-century situation in America which prompted Hawthorne's outburst at scribbling women. On the one hand, middle-class women of this period had begun to enjoy the leisure and education requisite for reading. On the other hand, they also had begun to experience an attenuation of opportunity, a peculiar "disestablishment."[13] As the American home was losing its importance in communal production, women found themselves increasingly more restricted to it. Privatizing the home and feminizing the family led, of course, precisely to the sexually unbalanced situation described by Chodorow: as female parents assumed almost exclusive responsibility for early child care, they perpetuated sex-marked developmental differences. Given features of the nineteenth-century middle-class situation, we should not be surprised that women were purchasing and reading texts in numbers previously unheard of, and that these texts differed in type from those read by men. Undoubtedly, this split in reading experiences produced yet further differences in the way women and men perceived themselves and the world. If we accept Leo Bersani's opinion that written "language doesn't merely describe identity but actually produces moral and perhaps even physical identity,"[14] we must conclude that "identities" produced during the nineteenth century through an immersion in literature split, most often, along sexual lines.

Nina Baym and others have charted basic characteristics of "the story" repeated over and over again in women's novels written and read during the mid-nineteenth century: "In essence, it is the story of a young girl who is deprived of the supports she had rightly or wrongly depended on to sustain her throughout life and is faced with the necessity of winning her own way in the world."[15] As Baym explains, this story both responded to socioeconomic conditions and ministered to the "inherent psychic needs" of its audience.[16] By the 1870's, however socioeconomic conditions and inherent psychic needs appear to have changed: "women's novels" of the type described by Baym failed to maintain popular interest. Looking at post-Civil War bestsellers, Baym suggests that "the feminine audience had become appreciative of a more androgynous literature. Works like *Ben Hur* and *In His Steps* . . . depict a community of men and women and imply general religious and social interests common to the sexes."[17] Although women readers undoubtedly helped put *Ben Hur* and *In His Steps* on the newly born bestseller charts, Baym shifts the terms of her argument somewhat by pointing to these texts. Earlier, Baym restricted her consideration to best-selling texts by and about women; obviously, both Lew Wallace's *Ben Hur* and Charles Sheldon's *In His Steps* fall outside Baym's original category. Are we to assume then that after 1870, texts *by* and *about* women no longer engaged a popular following *among* women? Because the nineteenth-century story articulated by Baym falls into disfavor, are we to believe that a specifically female story ceased to appeal?

On the contrary: it is the contention of this essay that women and men, in great numbers, continue to read different texts (or to read the same texts differently) and that a specific "woman's story" continues to motivate the sales of texts sold primarily to women. For evidence of the first contention we only need examine the shelf arrangement of a popular bookstore (Westerns on one side, romances on the other) or refer to the standard texts on popular culture: "The 'happy novels' satisfied one segment [read: women] of the popular market; the 'man story' appealed to another."[18] For evidence of the second, we must survey a range of twentieth-century "women's novels," paying attention to repeated plot structures, image patterns, and thematic concerns. The pages which follow provide a survey of five of the most famous twentieth-century American women's bestsellers—*Gone with the Wind, Forever Amber, Peyton Place, Valley of the Dolls,* and *Scruples*—all written by women, focused on women, and addressed primarily to women. Reading the texts carefully, we may construct a twentieth-century, white middle-class American "woman's story"—a revision of Baym's nineteenth-century plot outline, more in keeping with twentieth-century psychic needs. On the most obvious level, these texts portray women and men caught in webs of desire; they make their appeal to women interested in heterosexual romance. Less obviously (hence, more deviously and powerfully), the texts portray women and women caught in webs of desire; they appeal to women similarly caught. Repeatedly, the texts portray daughters who, while seeking recourse in the arms of father-lovers, are bound to their mothers by intense physical and emotional appetites. Nancy Chodorow's comments about girls in our society hold true for girls in the novels: "Girls cannot and do not 'reject' their mother and women in favor of their father and men, but remain in a bisexual triangle throughout childhood and puberty."[19] Caught in this triangle, daughter-heroines voice complaints shared by daughter-readers: it is mothers who condemn daughters to inhabit bodies capable of mothering (at best an equivocal operation); it is mothers who leave, failing to provide adequate nourishment; it is mothers who remain, exacting compensation for nourishment not provided. The story told in the bestsellers, then, is built upon a bisexual triangle, with tremendous psychic tension flowing between mother and daughter. This particular story helps account for the bestsellers' success; *Gone with the Wind, Forever Amber, Peyton Place, Valley of the Dolls,* and *Scruples* all allow a female reader to repeat the most ambivalent relationship of her childhood, that relationship with the woman upon whom she depended for sustenance and love, but from whom she eventually needed to distance herself.

On the basis of five bestsellers, I construct a twentieth-century American "woman's story." Various reservations may be raised with regard to this process. First: do five texts comprise a valid sample? A statistician might have doubts, at least until confronted with sales figures of the novels. All told, over 25,127,570 copies of *Gone with the Wind, Forever Amber, Peyton Place, Valley of the Dolls,* and *Scruples* have been sold. No one knows how many copies have been checked in and out of libraries or circulated among friends. Further, each novel gave birth to imitations which often addressed the same issues, appealed to the same audience, and enjoyed at least moderate success. Surely, these sales figures, especially when combined with "spin-off" sales figures, indicate a shared taste, a concensus.

We next must ask who shaped this consensus: do the novels owe their success primarily to women readers? Unfortunately, prior to the computer age, booksellers rarely kept demographic statistics; we do not possess a precise breakdown of the book buying public by sex. Thus, like Nina Baym working with nineteenth-century material, we must hypothesize an audience on the basis of advertising copy, review copy, and commentary from authors and their publishers. On all counts, evidence points to female consumers. Although the novels were advertised in magazines and newspapers with a general appeal, advertisements also appeared with some frequency in magazines geared specifically to women.[20] Review copy further supports the female-audience hypothesis. Many reviewers target women as the most appropriate or intended audience of the novel under review. For example, Robert Gutwilling, writing about the 1936 bestseller *Gone with the Wind,* comments: "It was a book written by a woman for women, and women embraced it. Women are traditionally the major book buyers in this country."[21] Stephen Vincent Benét also posits a female audience for *Gone with the Wind,* noting that Margaret Mitchell consistently centers a reader's interest "not upon the armies and the battles, the flags and the famous names, but upon that other world of women who heard the storm, waited it out, succumbed to it or rebuilt after it, according to their nature."[22] Similarly, William Du Bois predicts that on the basis of its heroine, *Forever Amber,* bestseller of 1944–45, will be a natural: "Anglo-Saxon booksellers, if they are honest, will confess that few characters in fiction are more beloved by female readers than the successful harlot."[23] Later reviewers continue to sing this refrain: Tom Nairn classifies Jacqueline Susann's *Valley of the Dolls* as "a sick woman's book, through and through"[24] and various reviewers cite *Scruples'*s Billy Ikehorn as a heroine sure to appeal to women.

Authors and publishers of the bestsellers seem to agree with their reviewers. Although Grace Metalious's 1956 bestseller *Peyton Place* certainly enticed readers of both sexes, Howard Goodkind, a Messner editor who worked on the *Peyton Place* publicity campaign, geared much of his advertising to housewives—women who, like Metalious, wanted to write, but unlike her, had not yet met with success.[25] Susann, possibly one of the best book marketers ever, also begins with a female audience (*Valley* "says something . . . and says it particularly to every woman"[26]) and assumes that male readers will be drawn in only later: "Men buy mostly non-fiction, history, biography. But if a book has that extra thing, if it's a real story, if it's excitement, then men will buy it, if only to find out why their wives sat up with it all night."[27] Curious husbands, however, have not purchased sufficient copies of *Valley* to mandate a reclassification of the novel. It remains a women's bestseller, at least according to its publisher, Bernard Geis, who estimates that the percentage of women readers of *Valley* ran "as high as 70 percent."[28] Discussing the intended audience for her 1978 bestseller *Scruples,* Judith Krantz ignores men altogether: "I wrote it because I realized that no one was writing the big, fun, entertainment book for women."[29] She further comments that *Scruples* "gives women a big bubble bath";[30] she fails to mention what it gives to men.

In foregrounding such comments I do not intend to suggest that men did not purchase and read *Gone with the Wind, Forever Amber, Peyton Place, Valley of the Dolls,* and *Scruples.* I do want to suggest, however, that the principal audience for these bestsellers is female. An occasional male may very well enjoy bubbles in Krantz's bathtub; I assign him the task of describing his enjoyment. In the pages which follow I treat the novels as "women's bestsellers"; I focus on female characters, concerns, and plot structures. In so doing, I hope to initiate discussion of both the texts and their readers. What do these novels say to women readers? In selecting the novels, what do these readers say to us? My questions imply a distance between me ("us") and the "woman reader"; in the sense that I critically analyze *Scruples,* I *am* at a distance from the woman who picks up a paperback copy of the novel at the grocery store, reads it through once quickly, and then passes it on to a friend. The essential experience of the novel, however—an experience of maternal loss and compensatory consumption—is the same both for me and for the casual reader;[31] we both partake of a reading process which allows us to transform specifically female wishes and fears into significance.[32] Reading *Scruples,* I engage in this process; analyzing *Scruples,* I describe the process. In other words, the distance I impose allows me to give voice to an experience that previously had no voice; it allows me to make conscious that which previously had been unconscious. Thus, in response to the sceptic who doubts that a critical reader is capable of representing the reading experience of thousands of women who have devoured *Scruples,* I maintain that although I may eat more slowly and more self-consciously than members of the female mass audience, we all eat the same meal.

While detailing the similarity of menu from one novel to the next, I would do an injustice to the individual novels if I failed to acknowledge their differences, differences arising out of their differing contexts. Each novel might be read as a historical document, revealing the tensions, struggles, wishes, and desires peculiar to its own period of popularity. Thus, we might consider ways in which *Gone with the Wind,* published in 1936, speaks to and about its Depression audience. Marion Morton begins such a consideration in an essay on the connections between Mitchell's audience and her Civil War characters. For example, Morton cites parallels between Scarlett O'Hara's fate and "that of millions of American women during the Depression, for whom scrimping and cutting corners became a way of life."[33] Similarly, we might note the ways in which *Peyton Place*, with its limited cast of characters all passionately engaged in interpersonal conflicts, accords with American middle-class society of the 1950's, which had withdrawn its attention from large landscapes to focus instead on a smaller family unit. Or again, we might look to *Scruples*, published in 1978, for its depiction of tensions peculiar to a late-twentieth-century audience of consumers caught in a system that demands ever more consumption.

In the pages which follow, however, I am less interested in differences from novel to novel and more interested in similarities. Thus, rather than pursuing a project along the lines of Morton's, I sacrifice consideration of context and change in favor of consideration of text and stability. Fifty-two years and a tremendous amount of history separate *Gone with the Wind* from *Scruples*, but these bestsellers, as well as *Forever Amber, Peyton Place,* and *Valley of the Dolls*, bear a marked resemblance to one another. The repeated features exceed simple chance; they testify, instead, to a familial linkage, a matrilineal tradition.

Notes

1. C. E. Frazer Clark, Jr., ed., *Letters of Hawthorne to William D. Ticknor* (New York: NCR Microcard Editions, 1972), p. 75. Quoted in Susan Geary, "The Domestic Novel as a Commercial Commodity: Making a Best Seller in the 1850's," *Bibliographical Society of America Papers* 70 (July 1976), p. 365.

2. James D. Hart, *The Popular Book: A History of America's Literary Taste* (Berkeley: University of California Press, 1961), p. 93.

3. Hart, p. 97.

4. See especially the comments of Henry Nash Smith in *Democracy and the Novel* (New York: Oxford University Press, 1978), pp. 1-15.

5. Smith notes that during the thirty years preceding the Civil War,

masculine and aristocratic values were supplanted by the leveling influences exerted by rapid increases in population and wealth, by the spread of free public schools, by the evangelical movements, and especially by the cultural influence of women, who for the first time were gaining enough leisure to have time to read, and enough education to enjoy and produce books. (P. 8)

6. Nina Baym explains that most male authors

assumed an audience of men as a matter of course, and reacted with distress and dismay as they discovered that to make a living by writing they would have to please female readers. Only three men before the Civil War enjoyed widespread success with women—Timothy Shay Arthur, Nathaniel P. Willis, and George Mitchell. (*Women's Fiction: A Guide to Novels by and about Women in America, 1820–1870* [Ithaca: Cornell University Press, 1978], p. 13)

7. For further discussion of "separate spheres," see Barbara Welter, "The Cult of True Womanhood 1820–1860," *American Quarterly* 18, no. 2 (Summer 1966), pp. 151-57; and Gerda Lerner, "The Lady and the Mill Girl," *Midcontinent American Studies Journal* 10, no. 1 (Spring 1969), pp. 5-15.

8. Norman N. Holland, *The Dynamics of Literary Response* (New York: Norton, 1975), p. 32.

9. Holland, p. 30.

10. Sigmund Freud, "Analysis Terminable and Interminable," in *The Standard Edition of the Complete Psychological Works of Sigmund Freud,* Vol. 23, trans. James Strachey (London: Hogarth, 1957), p. 233.

11. Nancy Chodorow, "Family Structure and Feminine Personality," in *Woman, Culture and Society,* ed. M. Rosaldo and L. Lamphere (Stanford: Stanford University Press, 1974), p. 47.

12. See especially Annette Kolodny, "A Map for Rereading: Or, Gender and the Interpretation of Literary Texts," *New Literary History* 11, no. 3 (Spring 1980), pp. 451-67; and Nelly Furman, "The Study of Women and Language," *Signs* 4, no. 1 (Autumn 1978), pp. 183-85.

13. Ann Douglas introduces this term in *The Feminization of American Culture* (New York: Avon Books, 1978). In her consideration of "The End of Mother Power" (pp. 55-64), she observes that as the home gave way to the factory as a site of financially productive endeavor, "the independent woman with a mind and life of her own slowly ceased to be considered of high value" (p. 59).

14. Leo Bersani, *A Future for Astyanax* (Boston: Little, Brown, 1976), p. 194.

15. Baym, p. 11.

16. Baym, p. 40.

17. Baym, p. 298.

18. Russell Nye, *The Unembarrassed Muse* (New York: Dial, 1970), p. 38. John Cawelti devotes somewhat more attention to the sexual split, but his conclusions are essentially the same as Nye's:

Appearing at all levels of culture [the adventure story] seems to appeal to all classes and types of person, though particularly to men. The feminine equivalent of the adventure story is the romance. This is not to say that women do not read adventure stories or that romances cannot be popular with men; there is no exclusive sexual property in these archetypes of fantasy. Nonetheless, the fact that most adventure formulas have male protagonists while most romances have female central characters does suggest a basic affinity between the different sexes and these two story types. (*Adventure, Mystery and Romance* [Chicago: University of Chicago Press, 1976], p. 41)

19. Nancy Chodorow, *The Reproduction of Mothering* (Berkeley: University of California Press, 1978), p. 41.

20. This trend is most obvious with the more recent novels. *Scruples,* for example, was reviewed in *Vogue* and excerpted in *Cosmopolitan* (March 1978). In addition, both Krantz and Susann made frequent guest appearances on daytime talk shows, the audience for which is composed principally of women.

21. Robert Gutwilling, "In History There's Never Been Anything Like It," *New York Times Book Review* (June 25, 1961), p. 6.

22. Stephen Vincent Benét, "Georgia Marches Through," *Saturday Review of Literature* 14 (July 4, 1936), p. 5.

23. William Du Bois, "Jumbo Romance of Restoration London," *New York Times Book Review* (Oct. 15, 1944), p. 7.

24. Tom Nairn, "Sex and Death," *New Statesman* (Mar. 8, 1968), p. 303.

25. Emily Toth, *Inside Peyton Place* (Garden City, New York: Doubleday, 1981), pp. 118-22.

26. Ken Purdy, "Valley of the Dollars," *Saturday Evening Post* (Feb. 24, 1968), p. 76.

27. Purdy, quoting Susann, p. 78.

28. Bernard Geis, letter to the author, Sept. 14, 1982.

29. Quoted in *Contemporary Authors, Vols. 81–84,* ed. Frances Locher (Detroit: Gale Research Co., 1979), p. 306.

30. Herbert Mitgang, quoting Krantz, "Behind the Bestsellers," *New York Times Book Review* (Mar. 19, 1978), p. 50.

31. I must add that the term "casual reader" may be a misnomer. Many women read these texts in a decidedly noncasual fashion; they immerse themselves in the novels and return to them time and time again. When I queried members of my family about their reading habits, one aunt admitted reading *Forever Amber* seven times and another aunt revealed that she rereads *Gone with the Wind* every year.

32. I do not want to suggest that these best-selling authors *consciously* manipulate primitive wishes and fears, nor that readers *consciously* select texts which allow for a psychically pleasurable transformation. It seems obvious to me, however, that the bestsellers succeed precisely because they provide readers with the possibility of reexperiencing, reworking, and mastering primitive fears and wishes—in this case, specifically female fears and wishes.

33. Marion J. Morton, " 'My Dear, I Don't Give a Damn': Scarlett O'Hara and the Great Depression," *Frontiers* 5, no. 3 (1981) p. 53.

— 1 —

Gone with the Wind: "And the Cupboard Was Bare"

"Oh, Miss Scarlett, now dat Miss Ellen's in de grabe, whut is we gwine ter do?"

—Margaret Mitchell, *Gone with the Wind*

This cathexis between mother and daughter—essential, distorted, misused—is the great unwritten story. Probably there is nothing in human nature more resonant with charges than the flow of energy between two biologically alike bodies, one of which has lain in amniotic bliss inside the other, one of which has labored to give birth to the other. The materials are here for the deepest mutuality and the most painful estrangement.

—Adrienne Rich, *Of Woman Born*

Early commentators on *Gone with the Wind* enjoy recounting its publishing history: how Margaret Mitchell refused to show Macmillan's Harold Latham her manuscript; how she changed her mind and presented herself at his hotel, almost engulfed by stacks of typed pages; how he purchased an extra suitcase to transport her many pages back to New York.[1] Of equal interest, however, is the history of this novel's birth: how it came to be written. In January, 1919, Margaret Mitchell, a freshman at Smith College, received a telegram calling her home to her dying mother. Before Mitchell arrived in Atlanta, however, her mother died, and the nineteen-year-old woman returned home to emptiness.[2] On her father's advice, Mitchell finished her second semester at Smith, then moved back to Atlanta to take her mother's place as "hostess and housekeeper of 1149 Peachtree Street."[3] In the seven years that followed, Mitchell cared for her father and brother, married twice, wrote for the *Atlanta Journal Sunday Magazine,* read most of the books in the Atlanta library, and sprained her ankle. This sprain, to the same ankle she seriously injured as a child, kept Mitchell confined to the small apartment she shared with her husband—and served as immediate impetus for the writing of her novel. As she notes in a 1936 letter to Mrs. Julia Collier Harris, "I was just writing to keep from worrying about never walking again."[4] In other words, to ward off a fear of loss, Mitchell fills potential voids—her time, her mind, her apartment— with words, thousands of words. The fear motivating Mitchell assumes particularly frightening proportions as it recalls an already experienced loss: that of the mother. The threat of never walking again, of falling into the role of dependent child, propels Mitchell into an alternative role: she becomes a word mother.

Almost without exception, when Mitchell discusses the genesis of her novel, she makes reference to some variety of maternal absence and compensatory production. In her most explicit statement about the birthing of *Gone with the Wind,* Mitchell points to Rhett Butler's famous remarks about the nature of survival in a world that often turns upside-down. Essentially, Rhett preaches a sermon of accommodation and flexibility, explaining that when the world is topsy-turvy, everyone must start over again, with nothing except their own cunning and strength.[5] Mitchell then observes: "in that paragraph lies the genesis of my book and that genesis lies years back when I was six years old and those words were said to me."[6] It was then that Mitchell's mother had taken her down the road toward Jonesboro, had shown her the ruins of old houses, and had talked to her "about the world those people had lived in, such a secure world, and how it had exploded beneath them. And she told me that my own world was going to explode under me, some day, and God help me if I didn't have some weapon to meet the new world."[7] Of course, in 1936, when Mitchell's novel was published, most readers assumed that Rhett offered advice for survival in the upside-down world of the Great Depression. Mitchell, however, wrote most of *Gone with the Wind* in the 1920's, prior to the national disaster; the novel grows out of a more personal disaster: the explosion of Mitchell's secure familial matrix, and the near collapse of the family home, which, following her mother's death, Mitchell had to keep from ruin.

Another rather curious gloss on forces associated with the production of *Gone with the Wind* occurs in a casual remark Mitchell addressed to a reviewer, Joseph Henry Jackson. Responding to Jackson's assessment of *Gone with the Wind* as yet another new novel about "destruction and rebirth and upheavals," Mitchell explains that she wrote her book "when the Great American Boom was at its height. . . . Everyone I knew had a car, a radio, an electric ice box and a baby that they were buying on time (everybody except me!)."[8] Mitchell's list (unbalanced somewhat by the final item), as well as her exclamatory parenthetical exception of self, calls attention to the woman whose house must be strangely bare, whose home lacks a baby. To fill these various spaces, then, Mitchell produces her novel, a novel preoccupied with improvident mothers, hungry daughters, and empty houses.

As if in accord with stereotypes of the good old days in a slow-moving South, Margaret Mitchell paces the opening chapters of *Gone with the Wind* so as to encourage a leisurely, almost sluggish, reading tempo. After an initial physical description of her heroine, Scarlett O'Hara, and a few sentences of dialogue between Scarlett and the Tarleton twins, Mitchell abandons Scarlett and indulges in a long-winded and apparently digressive pursuit of Stuart and Brent Tarleton. These two young men, killed early in the Civil War, play only very small roles in Mitchell's novel, and yet she devotes over half of the first chapter to describing their attempts to procure a good meal. Having been expelled from the University of Georgia, the twins are afraid to return home to their hot-tempered mother and expect Scarlett to extend a supper invitation. But Scarlett, upset with news of Ashley Wilkes's pending engagement to Melanie Hamilton, fails to play the Southern hostess, and the twins are left to their own devices. After expressing surprise over Scarlett's omission, Stuart and Brent go down a list of country families who might be expected to provide them with an evening meal. Finally, despite objections expressed by the twins' body servant, Jeems, about the fare to be found at Abe Wynder's, it is toward Wynder's that the boys direct their hungry stomachs. Still rather confused by Scarlett's apparent inhospitality, the Tarletons bring chapter one to a close with a short exchange:

"Look, Stu! Don't it seem like to you that Scarlett would have asked us to supper?"

"I kept thinking she would. . . . Why do you suppose. . . ." (Pp. 22-23)

While Stuart wonders about Scarlett, I wonder about Mitchell: why does she devote so much time to the problem of procuring a good supper? The question is not unimportant: in a letter to Mrs. E. L. Sullivan, Mitchell notes that she wrote her book "from the back to the front. That is, the last chapter first and the first chapter last."[9] Being so absolutely prescient, Mitchell may well have consciously crafted elements in her opening pages. Although conversation between the twins as well as commentary from the narrator intervene, the supper problem gives shape to the last half of chapter one; while the boys discuss activities in the neighborhood, while the narrator fleshes out their discussion with more historical details, hunger pangs quicken and Stu and Brent return, continually, to one topic: food. Also, with each return, a connection between food and women is forged. Ideally, mother Beatrice Tarleton should provide for her sons' sustenance, but, given her temper and their fall from grace, the twins know they had better look elsewhere, to some other woman. Scarlett O'Hara, seated on the porch of an obviously productive plantation, would seem to offer Brent and Stu access to a land of plenty. Certainly, Scarlett herself is surrounded by examples of "good mothers": women who occupy them-selves in procuring food for others. While Scarlett flirts with the twins, her mother Ellen goes to the smokehouse to gather provisions for the homecoming hands, and her nurse, Mammy, orders Pork to lay out plates for the twins, assuming that Scarlett will invite them to supper. Despite these models, despite broad hints from the twins, Scarlett, like Mrs. Tarleton, fails to fill these children's stomachs. Confused, annoyed, and hungry, Stuart and Brent contemplate other alternatives, but in each case a woman bars the way to a comfortable supper: Stuart prefers to avoid India Wilkes, to whom he had paid court and then abandoned, and both boys dislike the Yankee stepmother of Cade and Calvert. The two young men finally must turn to another of their own sex, Abe Wynder, and, as Jeems suggests, this turn indicates that matters have come to a sorry state indeed.

Certainly, Mitchell treats the Tarletons' quest in a light-hearted and humorous fashion, but as she draws upon elements from basic child-hood nightmares in structuring her account (to be hungry, to be denied food from the mother), she touches upon primitive fears and frustra-tions. If chapter one, usually read as a leisurely introduction to the ways of Southern belles and beaux, actually initiates a more complex and decidedly ambivalent representation of frustrations attendant upon a sense of maternal deficiency, chapters two through four—chapters, again, most often read as mere staging prior to more important scenes— elaborate this representation, subtly, deviously: once more, mothers fail to meet children's nutritional needs. In chapter two, for example, Scarlett intercepts her father on his way home from the Wilkes's plantation, learns that her beloved Ashley is to marry Melanie, and then returns to Tara for supper. Approaching the house, Scarlett meets her mother, who has been called away to nurse a neighbor. Ellen pats Scarlett's cheek and, in one of the remarkably few exchanges between mother and daughter to which we are privy, requests that Scarlett take her place at the table. Although Ellen, unlike Beatrice Tarleton, makes sure that the table is laden with food before she leaves, she *does* leave, thereby failing to supply daughter Scarlett with the emotional sustenance she so much desires at this point. Despite plentiful fried chicken, hot buttered biscuits, and yams, this meal is incomplete: Scarlett cannot fill Ellen O'Hara's place. Thus, on an emotional level, chapter two repeats the situation of chapter one.

Relating the specific nature of Ellen's nursing errand, Mitchell composes further variations on the theme of maternal insufficiency. Ellen tells Gerald that there is illness at the Slattery house; Emmie Slattery's newborn baby is dying and must be baptized. Why does this baby die? Mitchell specifies no cause—no cause except female inadequacy; as Emmie provides no father for her child, it is unlikely that she will provide for it in other ways. So closely linked to birth, this baby's death serves as warning: once a mother thrusts her child from the all-provident womb, death is around the corner.

In the first four chapters of *Gone with the Wind,* Mitchell introduces image clusters which, throughout the remainder of her novel, she will associate with concepts of the maternal. Paying attention to these image clusters, I find myself in disagreement with generally accepted critical assessments of *Gone with the Wind* as romanticized history. Repeatedly, reviewers chastise Mitchell for her sun-drenched, rose-colored portrait of life on an antebellum Southern plantation (Floyd Watkins complains that "*Gone with the Wind* is a world without sweat, except for that caused by the Yankees").[10] These reviewers have spent, perhaps, too much time in the sun themselves; they see only certain highlights of Mitchell's novel. As should be apparent from discussion on preceding pages, Mitchell, far from proposing that life always runs smoothly, draws upon some of our most primitive fears to suggest that even everyday events may prompt responses of extreme ambivalence. If, instead of approaching the novel as Civil War history, we read it as a woman's personal history, charges of antebellum falsification become irrelevant, and we come closer to an understanding of the power that this best-selling novel exerts over its female readers. Further, by focusing more intently on the structures of Scarlett's experience, we call into question another standard assessment of *Gone with the Wind:* that it appeals to female buyers because it is a formulaic romance of the "and-he-still-pursued-her" variety.[11] Certainly, Mitchell makes use of hero/heroine romance in *Gone with the Wind,* but, as the first four chapters intimate and the remainder of the novel substantiates, a more fundamental romance—hence, more carefully hidden and more powerfully frustrated—occurs between Scarlett and her mother.

In the pages that follow, I want to elaborate on image clusters and thematic associations introduced in the first four chapters of *Gone with the Wind* as they appear in two later, especially important scene sequences: the first includes the birth of Melanie's baby, Scarlett's flight to Tara, her arrival at an empty house; the second, the death of Melanie, Scarlett's flight to Rhett, and her decision to return to the house that has disappointed her in the past. Even in quick overview, it should be apparent that the sequences are patterned on similar templates: having witnessed the termination of a pregnancy more closely associated with death than life, Scarlett flees; in her flight she initially looks to a male for aid but soon, rejected by him, she turns toward a mother whose womb, in Scarlett's imagination, is not defiled by death and disappointment. Having been attentive to notes of disappointment and frustration in the first four chapters, we should not be surprised at the outcome of the two sequences here: Scarlett's dream of sheltering maternal space becomes a nightmare of absence. It is this nightmare, experienced by female readers in life and re-experienced in the text, that accounts, at least in good part, for the power of *Gone with the Wind.*

Suffering intense labor pains, Francesca Valensky, a character in Judith Krantz's 1980 bestseller, *Princess Daisy,* requests drugs from her doctor. He explains that drugs might affect the soon-to-be-born baby and Francesca goes pale with terror: "Like generations of American women, her idea of childbirth without drugs was firmly based on the long and fatal agony of Melanie Wilkes in *Gone with the Wind.*"[12] Krantz's attribution of mythic power to the scene from *Gone with the*

Wind is no exaggeration; I remember breathlessly reading those pages as a young girl and deciding to remain safely childless all my life. What is the source of power here? How does the scene work?

First, of course, is Mitchell's insistence upon an association of birth with death. Melanie suggests this association when she pleads with Scarlett to take her baby if Melly should die while giving birth to it. Despite Scarlett's assertion that Melanie is not going to die and that all first-time mothers experience this same fear, the possibility of death has been raised, and as Melanie's pains become more intense, the possibility becomes more frightening. Further, Melanie's attempt to give her child life occurs in the midst of a much larger context of death: dying and wounded soldiers crowd the streets of Atlanta. Scarlett, seeking the doctor who has promised to assist in what looks to be a difficult delivery, confronts death directly. As she pushes through the tangle of ambulances, dust clouds, stretcher bearers, in search of Dr. Meade, she comes in view of the depot. There, in the fierce heat, lay hundreds of dead and dying soldiers; Scarlett steps into the midst of "an inferno of pain and smell and noise" (p. 300). When Scarlett finally finds Dr. Meade, she finds a man whose clothing is as red as a butcher's, whose hair is matted with blood, and whose duty lies with dying men rather than birthing women. Terrified, Scarlett pleads that the doctor leave a scene of death for a very similar scene; like these men, Melanie lies writhing, moaning, screaming, beset by flies and foul odors. But the doctor will not come, and Scarlett must make her way back through the mad crowd alone.

Here, in Scarlett's search, Scarlett's fear and agony, is the true nightmare of these chapters—much more so than in Melanie's pain. As readers we are drawn more fully into Scarlett's role, that of responsible but helpless witness, than we are to Melly's, that of rather unconscious principal. We follow Scarlett as she trades the oppression of Melanie's bedroom for the oppression of streets crowded with bodies, then climbs back up the stairs to Melanie's room to reassume her position by Melanie's side without the hope of professional assistance. The horrors experienced by Scarlett are the horrors of a dreamer caught in a nightmare that just gets worse: first, the peculiar stillness and heat of the lying-in chamber (Scarlett feels trapped in a prison of timeless, sweating darkness), then the wild madness of the streets (where a formerly staid matron, Mrs. Elsing, careens through the crowd, and drunken, garishly dressed women hang on the arms of soldiers yet drunker than they), then a return to the closeness of Melanie's room, where Scarlett comes to feel that she would prefer anything to being a "helpless witness to such pain" (p. 300). Finally, having given birth to her baby, Melanie falls asleep; Scarlett, the deliverer, remains awake, unable to close her eyes after having witnessed such horrors. When Scarlett thinks back to her own pregnancy and the birth of her son Wade, she can remember next to nothing, but now, having been involved in this "nightmare of screaming pain and ignorant midwifery," Scarlett will not be able to forget—just as we, reader-witnesses, also will not be able to forget. Skillfully, Mitchell both increases the horror of this scene and allocates this horror to Scarlett as she denies us a full account of the actual delivery, providing us instead with fragments from Scarlett's tortured memory of her reluctant participation as midwife.

One of the events that contributes to the scene's effect—an event so basic that it almost passes without comment—is the actual separation of child from mother. Dr. Meade touches upon this necessary separation in his extremely abbreviated instructions to Scarlett: "There's nothing much to bringing a baby. Just tie up the cord" (p. 302). Tying, however, implies cutting, and cutting most forcefully affects Scarlett, a woman still tied as an emotional dependent to her own mother. Thus, almost immediately after the severing of Beau from his mother, Scarlett determines upon a return to her mother. Sitting on the porch trying to renew her strength, Scarlett sees flames, realizes Atlanta is on fire and panics: "She was a child and mad with fright and she wanted to bury her head in her mother's lap and shut out this sight" (p. 312). The desire is one expressed by Scarlett over and over again: to return to the comfort of Ellen's lap, Mammy's arms; to be enclosed within a protective maternal space. Interestingly, Scarlett's restatement of the desire here—"to bury her head in her mother's lap and shut out this sight"—is sparked most directly by her vision of Atlanta in flames, but also must be prompted by her earlier vision of child separated from mother. Her yearning for Ellen is to be read as an attempt to deny the fact of this separation.

Acting upon her desire, Scarlett commandeers Rhett and the two of them, along with Melanie, Beau, Prissy, and Wade, start for Tara. Momentarily, the nightmarish aspects of Scarlett's day appear to abate; Rhett takes charge. But not far outside Atlanta, Rhett, like Dr. Meade (the other man who abandons Scarlett when she calls upon him for assistance), chooses to align himself with men and war, as distinguished from women and houses. Scarlett once again falls into a horror-filled landscape and events during the night seem to mirror, inversely, those during the day: the bright light and oppressive heat of the September day give way to darkness and cold fear as Scarlett, crazily, pilots four children back to an originary space.

The charm that Scarlett calls upon, the prod with which she forces herself forward, is Ellen—for Scarlett, the embodiment of security and stability. As a child, Scarlett confused her mother with the Virgin Mary and she sees no reason to right this confusion as she grows older; for Scarlett, Ellen continues to represent a heavenly security. Now, working her way homeward, burdened with the knowledge of Ellen's sickness, Scarlett further obfuscates boundaries by pushing for an identification between Ellen and Ellen's house: Tara is the Heaven/ haven over which Ellen presides. With each weary step, Scarlett yokes the person and place together more firmly: she wants to run to get "closer to Tara and to Mother" (p. 330) and fears it will be hours "before she knew if Tara still stood and if Ellen were there" (p. 330). Ironically, it is this yoking that must undermine Scarlett's faith, for, as she draws near Tara, the landscape suggests that both heaven and its inhabitants have been destroyed: the countryside looks "like the familiar and dear face of *a mother,* beautiful and quiet at last, after death agonies" (p. 331; my italics). The simile is ominous, not so much because it forecasts Ellen's death, but because it intensifies associations between mothers and death; using the indefinite article "a" Mitchell allows us to see this face as belonging not only to Ellen, Scarlett's mother, but to *any* mother, perhaps to our own mothers. Thus, for example, the desolated landscape also may be linked to Melly, the woman who most recently has become a mother and whose face, tortured with the agonies of labor pains, now resembles that of a woman who has seen death and rests peacefully. Having forged specific connections between Ellen and the land, Mitchell moves toward non-specification, thereby drawing a more generalized population of daughters/readers into Scarlett's nightmare.

And the nightmare continues. After a night and a day, Scarlett and her charges arrive at Tara. Scarlett peers up "the long tunnel of darkness" so as to discern whether or not Tara still stands; she wonders if the gloomy darkness hides the "dear white walls" of Tara, or if it "mercifully conceal[s] such a horror as the MacIntosh house" (p. 336).

The passage expresses fear of the maternal body; what horrors confront the child who strains her eyes to peer up a "tunnel of darkness"? Obviously, Scarlett has had to do just this while performing her function as midwife for Melanie. As the shadowy outlines of her home grow more distinct, Scarlett, hoping to hug the walls themselves, starts to rush forward but then senses something is wrong: an "eerie quiet" hangs over the plantation. Gerald appears on the verandah, but he too is peculiarly silent. When Scarlett asks about her mother and sisters, Gerald replies that Scarlett's sisters are doing well. Terrified, Scarlett cannot utter the question that must be asked, the question that might resolve "the frightening riddle of Tara's silence." Finally, Gerald speaks:

> "Your mother—" he said and stopped.
> "And—Mother?"
> "Your mother died yesterday." (P. 338)

Occurring a third of the way through the novel, this passage marks one of its climaxes. Suddenly, fears and premonitions from the past few days fall together, find a focus. For Scarlett, Tara is empty: the promise of maternal presence at the end of the tunnel has been betrayed. Looking for Ellen's arms, Scarlett finds only blank walls, dead ends. The child returns home to discover that there is no home, that the cord has been cut, that she is no longer a child. Protesting against these truths, Scarlett wishes for someone "in whose lap she could lay her head, someone on whose shoulders she could rest her burdens" (p. 345). As if in response to Scarlett's wish, Dilcey, with large bronze breasts exposed, enters the room, nursing Melanie's baby. Beau sucks greedily. Essentially, Scarlett would like to do the same; it is nourishment (of various kinds) from mama's breast that the "hongry chile" Scarlett craves. Dilcey's arrival presages, for Scarlett, a possible reprieve; although the mother who gave birth to her is dead, the mother who nursed her yet lives. Thus, when Scarlett hears Mammy's heavy tread, she runs to her and lays her head on Mammy's breasts. "Here was something of stability, thought Scarlett, something of the old life that was unchanging" (p. 346). Because of the structure of plantation life in the antebellum South, Scarlett actually has two mothers, and she hopes to find the stable presence she requires in Mammy, now that Ellen has failed her. But, as Mitchell records, Mammy's first words to Scarlett "dispelled this illusion": "Mammy's chile is home! Oh, Miss Scarlett, now dat Miss Ellen's in de grabe, whut is we gwine ter do?" (p. 346). Obviously, Mammy is more of a child than Scarlett, and the latter, disappointed once more, realizes that she must assume responsibility for yet another orphan.

The child Scarlett receives a further push toward adulthood when Dilcey informs her that as Ellen lay on her death bed, she did not ask for any family members but, rather, cried for someone named Philippe. Unaware of a Philippe in Ellen's past, Scarlett sadly perceives the limitation of her perception of Ellen: rents appear in a formerly whole (if imaginary) fabric. These rents are realized graphically as Scarlett, leaving the sickroom in which her mother has died and her two sisters combat the raging fever of typhus, looks out the window of Tara. The plantation stretches before her, *"like a body bleeding under her eyes, like her own body, slowly bleeding"* (p. 349; my italics). Up to this point, Mitchell consistently has called upon maternal bodies to function as vehicle in land similes; she now requires that daughter Scarlett assume the position previously held by Ellen. In her movement from the generalized "a body" to the more specific attribution "her own body," Mitchell underscores Scarlett's reluctance to accept this burden. Also, in coloring this body with blood, Mitchell suggests that on a purely physical level, Scarlett, possessed of a body that bleeds/menstruates, is as capable as Ellen of assuming maternal burdens.

Capable she is. Here we come to another extremely potent ingredient in Scarlett's character that prompts strong reader response. We are drawn to Scarlett not only because we share her desire to be cared for, to realize a perfectly stable relationship with an all-provident mother, but also because once Scarlett's desire is denied, she shows herself capable of caring for herself. Surrounded by children (everyone on the plantation, including her father, depends upon her; they look to her with eyes filled with helplessness), Scarlett pursues the course of an adult—of a mother.[13] As mentioned earlier, one of the cardinal duties of mothers in *Gone with the Wind* is to provide food, and some of Scarlett's very first efforts, once informed of her mother's death, are directed to this end. Having eaten very little during the past two days, Scarlett asks Pork if there is food in the house, only to be told that the Yankees have taken everything. She then gives evidence of her abilities as provider; where Pork assumes the plantation to be barren, Scarlett can suggest spots of fertility: the sweet potato hills and scuppernong arbor may furnish immediate food and drink.

In the days that follow, Scarlett must forage further for supplies. Mitchell's depiction of Scarlett ravaging the slave quarter gardens at Twelve Oaks, biting into a dirty radish, vomiting, and then making her vow to heaven—"I'm never going to be hungry again" (p. 357)—affects us powerfully as it presents us with a woman confronting an elementary fear of childhood: what happens when mother's cupboards are bare? But this depiction is double-edged; it conveys the intensity both of Scarlett's hunger and of her will to live. As Scarlett lies prostrate in the dirt, she determines that there is no going back to the past (mother Ellen *is* dead) and that she must go forward. Propelled by this determination, Scarlett rises and settles her basket, heavy with turnips and cabbages, across her arm. This act is significant: Scarlett's willingness to shoulder a basket containing food for the "children" at Tara indicates her assumption of a maternal responsibility. The basket cuts into her flesh, as does the responsibility. Although Scarlett manages to put apples, yams, peanuts, and milk on the table, she is ever preoccupied with the food problem; prodded by demands from her empty stomach, Scarlett restricts her thoughts to "food and how to get it" (p. 357). Despite her prohibition against musing on the past, Scarlett often wakes to find herself dreaming of meals from the old days. Mitchell, in a paragraph that almost drips off the page, allows Scarlett to reminisce about rolls, corn muffins, ham, fried chicken, collards, all "dripping butter, all at one meal" (p. 358).

Resenting the demands of her own stomach, Scarlett comes to resent those who look up to her with hunger in their eyes. In an exchange between Scarlett and her two convalescent sisters, Mitchell portrays this resentment as that which so often occurs between a mother and her children. Tired of being the provider, the bad mother (the step-mother or wicked witch of fairy tale) expresses her ambivalence in threats. Here, Scarlett outlines the work she expects Suellen and Careen to do once they have recovered. They look at her "as if she were a hobgoblin." When Careen protests that she cannot split kindling because it would ruin her hands, Scarlett pushes her own blistered and calloused palms toward Careen and crows like a witch. Members of the household remark upon Scarlett's transformation, and Scarlett herself is not oblivious to the change that prompts her to take pleasure in bullying the Negroes and harrowing the feelings of her sisters. But she cannot go back; the change is a result, in part, of a changed perception of her mother, whose teaching about antebellum proprieties proves inadequate for life during and after the war. Acting as the bad mother, Scarlett avenges herself on the good mother who, finally, wasn't good enough.

When Scarlett complains that nothing Ellen has taught her is of any help and then cries out that her mother was wrong, all wrong, she appears to have lost all moorings. But such is not the case: Tara, unlike the occupant who cast her charm over its acres, still stands. The plantation originally appeals to Scarlett because she associates it with Ellen, but once Ellen has left, Tara retains its hold; while Scarlett changes in many ways, her love for the land remains unchanged. Interestingly, Scarlett incorporates the land; as she loves it, it becomes *part of her.* Of course, it is far easier to incorporate land (which does not go away) than mothers (who do). Finally, however, Scarlett manages to keep her mother in place by reassociating her with the land. Looking over the trampled acres of Tara, Scarlett recalls a comment from her father: he observed that to the Irish, land on which they live "is like their mother" (p. 362).[14] Thus, by making the land live, Scarlett makes Ellen live as well—but safely, within the confines of Scarlett's own mind.

Before proceeding to an analysis of the final scenes from *Gone with the Wind* I want to backtrack briefly and call attention to certain aspects of Scarlett's relationship to Melanie. In chapter one we are told that Scarlett detests Melanie because the latter is to marry Ashley Wilkes, a man Scarlett has chosen as her own particular beau. Scarlett's infatuation with Ashley fuels the flames of her dislike for Ashley's wife up until the birth of Ashley's and Melanie's child, at which time Scarlett's feeling becomes more complex. This feeling takes on qualities of Scarlett's response to her mother, toward all mothers. Prior to the birth scene, Mitchell links Melanie and Ellen as "great ladies" in the Southern tradition; they share a belief in the goodness of humankind and a willingness to act on this belief.[15] But Scarlett refuses to see similarities between Melanie and Ellen; Rhett enumerates Melanie's qualities to Scarlett, Scarlett enumerates Ellen's qualities to Rhett, and Scarlett cannot hear the overlap. Mitchell will not allow us such deafness, however; she structures her story so as to insist on a coincidence of the two women and of Scarlett's responses to them. For example, as Scarlett, in Atlanta, waits for Melanie to give birth, she receives a note from Gerald, saying that Ellen, at Tara, is ill. Frantic, Scarlett curses Melanie, prays for Ellen, and, within the space of three sentences, envisions both of them dead:

> "Oh, Mother! Mother! Don't die! Why don't this baby ever come? . . . Dear God! Suppose she should die! Melanie dead. Melanie dead." (Pp. 288-89)

Although we know the pronoun "she" refers to Melanie (because of Scarlett's reference to the baby), its grammatical antecedent is "mother": the two mothers collapse together, and they do so under the sign of Death. Mitchell enforces this conjunction with a seemingly obvious parallelism in plot: Melanie gives birth on the day Ellen dies. Once at Tara, Melanie assumes the role most recently and reluctantly held by Ellen—that of the overextended mother: frail, emaciated, and care-worn. Thus, if Ellen's death affects a change in Scarlett, it also affects a change in Scarlett's relationship to Melanie, the woman who most resembles Ellen. Scarlett begins to call upon Melanie at those times she might have called upon Ellen, and Melanie answers, until she, like Ellen, deserts her children.

And so we come to the second sequence of scenes, bearing uncanny resemblance to the sequence discussed above, but paced at an accelerated speed. Like the first sequence, the second begins with Scarlett's participation in the final stages of Melanie's pregnancy—presumably, a life process, but a life process linked with death. When Ellen falls ill at Tara, Scarlett is in Atlanta; now, when Melanie falls ill in Atlanta, Scarlett is in Marietta. Both times she must make a return trip in fear, fear of the absence that might confront her at the end of her trip.[16] Arriving in the depot, Scarlett learns that Melanie still lives, but that she has had a miscarriage. When Scarlett protests to Rhett that the doctor had warned Melanie that another pregnancy would put her in the grave, Rhett replies that it has done so. Rhett's simple reply is chilling, as it summarizes the interaction between mothers and children in this novel: mothers either kill or are killed by their offspring. Scarlett rushes to Melanie's bedroom, which, in its darkness and stillness, must remind us of another bedroom: that in which Melanie gave birth to Beau. To reinforce this memory, Melanie makes reference to her first pregnancy, when she first asked Scarlett to care for Beau if anything should happen to her. And Scarlett's memory carries her back to the time she will never be able to forget; she remembers the heat of that day, her terror, Melanie's terror, and finally, she remembers her hatred of Melanie, and her wish that Melanie might die (p. 840). The memory of hatred prompts a childish feeling of guilt: the child, who has experienced ambivalence toward her mother, assumes responsibility for her death. Mitchell allows for an intensification of this guilt as she plays with yet one other connection between the two scenes: in the first, Scarlett wishes that Melanie's pregnancy will end with an early delivery; in the second, this wish is realized, as Melanie's pregnancy comes to term far too early, and with it, Melanie's life.

Melanie's death affects Scarlett in much the same way as Ellen's death does. First, Scarlett finds that she must assume maternal responsibility for orphans, of all ages, left by the other woman: on her deathbed, Melanie wills the care of her son and husband to Scarlett. Second, and more important, Scarlett sees that this woman who dies has been a tower of strength for her, that this woman's love has sheltered her in numerous unacknowledged ways.[17] The impact of this realization is shattering; Scarlett relives the death of her mother. For this lost child, it is as if Ellen lies behind Melanie's bedroom door; Scarlett once again confronts the chaos and terror of a world suddenly empty, a world without supports. At this point, Mitchell accelerates patterns of repetition, intensifies the nightmare that threatens to engulf us as well as Scarlett. Participating in the delivery process at the end of Melanie's first pregnancy, Scarlett confronts separation: child is cut from mother. Here, again, at the end of a pregnancy, Scarlett confronts separation, although this time it is the separation of death. Terrified, Scarlett seeks compensatory union in the arms of Ashley and Rhett. When she rushes to Ashley, then to Rhett, we share her feeling of *déjà vu;* she senses that she has been in this place before, has encountered these circumstances before. Of course, the circumstances in which she finds herself are those of her flight from Atlanta to Tara, and those of a nightmare, oft-repeated, which begins to haunt Scarlett following this flight. In the nightmare, Scarlett, confronted with the emptiness of Tara, does not know where to turn; she runs frantically and blindly through a thick fog, sobbing, crying, looking for someone or something capable of sheltering her. In episodes preceding the onset of this nightmare, Scarlett had called upon two men for aid: Dr. Meade and Rhett. Both, in their own ways, had failed her. Here, reliving the nightmare, Scarlett once again calls on two men, Ashley and Rhett, and once again, in different ways, they cannot respond. Ashley proves to be a child himself, a fantasy created by the very young Scarlett, and Rhett—Rhett gives up the battle for the future and joins those who look to the past.

Overcome with pain following the death of Melanie and the destruc- · tion of her illusions about Ashley, Scarlett refuses to remain in the Wilkes's house and determines that she must go home. This time, however, "home" is not Tara, but rather, a house on Peachtree Street in Atlanta, a house she shares with a husband, instead of a mother. In other words, Scarlett's center of security and stability has undergone a shift most often associated with heterosexual maturation. As she runs, she realizes that when she ran to Ellen, "she had found security gone, all strength, all wisdom, all loving tenderness, all understanding gone" (p. 849)—and she imagines that now, running to Rhett, she will find these things in his strong arms and complete understanding. Does Scarlett ever distinguish Rhett from Ellen? Does her feeling for Rhett differ from her feeling for Ellen: the feeling of a child who repeatedly and petulantly denies the fact of separation? Mitchell's prose will not allow us to escape these questions, as she introduces key words and phrases from Scarlett's original flight here. Further, as Mitchell recalls the earlier nightmare, I recall a question posed by Rhett after he listens to Scarlett describe her nightmare, and Rhett's question may point to an answer to the questions above. He asks Scarlett if she hunts for a person or a thing and Scarlett replies that she doesn't know. The exchange is significant: Rhett hopes that Scarlett may turn to him, may see that as one unique human being, he offers her refuge; while Scarlett, still engaged in an impossible quest for an all-encompassing union with the maternal (realized either as mother or as mother's house), cannot distinguish the most vague outlines of individuation. Although Scarlett now specifies Rhett as the object of her hunt, the hunt itself resembles, too closely, that for the mother's body.[18]

Such a reading is borne out in subsequent events. When Scarlett arrives at the house on Peachtree Street, it is not empty, but it might as well be: the man who sits inside withdraws his love from her, excuses himself from her life. Sure, as the small child is sure, that love is to be given on demand, Scarlett insists that Rhett open his arms to her, offer a breast on which she may lay her head. Rhett's refusal reenacts a mother's refusal, finally, to participate in the child's vision of her as simple extension rather than separate individual. While Scarlett must accept the fact of Rhett's departure, she cannot accept the fact of disconnection: disappointed by Rhett, Scarlett will return, once again, to maternal origins. Certainly, mother Ellen disappoints her daughter, but because Scarlett, immediately following Ellen's death, embarks on a process of generalization and obfuscation whereby land and house are identified with mother, she now perceives Tara as a possible locus for reunification, nondifferentiation, and wholeness. Thus, when Scarlett, on the final page of the novel, determines that she will go home, the home in question is not the home which she, only a few hours earlier on this same evening, set as her goal. Further, the embrace that she now craves is not that of Rhett, but, characteristically, that of a mother: Mammy. Scarlett imagines that Mammy will be at Tara and this ever-unsatisfied child wants Mammy desperately, just as when she was a little girl and had "wanted the broad bosom on which to lay her head. . . . Mammy, the last link with the old days"(p. 862).

Mammy may very well be at Tara, just as she was at Tara following Ellen's death but now, as then, she cannot possibly meet Scarlett's expectations. Again, by suggesting a repetition of previous scenes, Mitchell undermines belief in some past wholeness. Following Ellen's death, Scarlett lays her head on Mammy's broad sagging breasts and thinks, "here was something of stability . . . something of the old life that was unchanging" (p. 346). But Mammy's first words have to do with "weary loads" and Scarlett's illusions of stability are dispelled, just as they must be dispelled in her second return to Tara. Thus, although I enjoy Leslie Fiedler's analysis of the final pages of *Gone with the Wind*—he notes that when Scarlett decides to return to Tara only " 'Mammy' remains, as she must, since 'home' is where she has always been, will always be"[19]—I sense that Fiedler operates here under the same illusion as Scarlett. The fact is, *Gone with the Wind* works to show us that Mammys have *not* always been at home, will *not* always be at home. We may desire Mammy as a stable presence but Mitchell, from the first pages of her novel on, denies the possible realization of this desire: Ellen's absence at the dinner table presages later, more permanent absence.

Interestingly, the way Mitchell exposes the necessary failure of Scarlett's attempt to repeat, in the future, a golden union that never even existed in the past, also may be read as a more general exposure of imaginary constructions of the past as a golden age. The novel discloses the dangers in an imaginary identification of any particular age—in the life of an individual or of a nation—as a time of wholeness. Reading the novel in this way, we may challenge those reviewers who criticize *Gone with the Wind* for being a simple-minded paean to the pre-Civil War South. When Robert Gutwilling in *New York Times Book Review* comments,

> The book will be read as long as we keep escaping back to our ancestors and our past, although it tells us nothing significant about either. . . . It permits us the luxury of looking back at our crucial experience without insisting that we face up to the facts and implications of the Civil War, why it was fought and what was decided[20]

we must ask to whose "past," whose "crucial experience," Gutwilling refers. If he were to position himself among a group of female readers looking back at "our" crucial personal experiences represented in this text, he would not be able to dismiss *Gone with the Wind* as a work which "tells us nothing significant." Further, while the novel may not insist that we "face up to the facts and implications of *the* Civil War," it does encourage us to confront facts and implications of *a* civil war: that waged within the private citizen, within the psyche of the female child.

It is this battle, available as highly charged unconscious fantasy, which accounts in large part for the popularity of *Gone with the Wind*. Certainly, we may attribute the novel's appeal to various factors operating on a conscious level. Marion Morton, for example, offers a very interesting analysis of *Gone with the Wind* as a phenomenon of the thirties. She notes first that when Scarlett returns to a barren plantation, "her fate is like that of millions of American women during the Depression, for whom scrimping and cutting corners became a way of life";[21] and second, that when Scarlett finally loses Rhett, the novel "assure[s] its readers that the world could again be orderly, not by restoring wealth and power but by putting women like Scarlett in their rightful places."[22] Morton's interpretation of *Gone with the Wind*'s popularity in the thirties is convincing, but it does not explain why the novel continues to sell, why women like myself—growing up in the fifties and sixties—find it almost impossible to put down. For such an explanation, we must delve beneath that which is conscious, adult, and intellectual, to the realm of fantasy: "unconscious, infantile, and fraught with emotion."[23] The fantasy operating in *Gone with the Wind*— operating on both the novel's author and on us, its readers—engages us in repeated cycles of desire and denial: desire for an imaginary all-provident mother, denial of her actual existence.

The novel allows us, and Mitchell, to look back, at the same time that it comments on the futility of doing so. When Scarlett scrounges for food at Twelve Oaks, when she vows she will never be hungry again, she also pledges that as there is no going back, she is going forward. Mitchell then comments that although countless "bitter-eyed" Southern women would look backward, "to dead times, to dead men, evoking memories that hurt and were futile" (p. 356), Scarlett was not among them; she was never to look back. Curiously, Mitchell makes no mention of dead women, and her omission is significant as it suggests her own unconscious involvement in this particular form of looking back. Further, if Mitchell were to include dead women in her list, she would find herself caught in a contradiction: the novel shows that Scarlett repeatedly looks back, back to her mother. Reading *Gone with the Wind*, we may do the same, until the novel calls us up, depicting the nightmare that might be if we assume our reverie is reality. The all-provident mother-myth that *Gone with the Wind* destroys is beautiful; the novel succeeds because Mitchell so fully conveys both this beauty and its falseness.

Notes

1. See, for example, Ralph McGill, "*Gone with the Wind,* the Story behind the Story," *Red Barrel* 15 (Sept. 1936), pp. 14-20; and Faith Baldwin, "The Woman Who Wrote *Gone with the Wind,*" *Pictorial Review* 28 (Mar. 1937), pp. 4, 69-70, 72.

2. Finis Farr, *Margaret Mitchell of Atlanta* (New York: Morrow, 1965), p. 44.

3. Farr, p. 49. See also letter to Dr. Charles E. Mayo, August 22, 1936, in *Margaret Mitchell's "Gone with the Wind" Letters: 1936-1946,* ed. Richard Harwell (New York: Macmillan Book Co., 1976), pp. 54-55 (henceforth referenced simply as *Letters*). Writing to Mayo, Mitchell notes that although she started out to be a psychiatrist, she "was forced to leave college when my

mother died as I was the only daughter in the family, and was needed at home to keep house."

4. *Letters,* p. 5.

5. Rhett's speech is on p. 644 of Mitchell's *Gone with the Wind* (New York: Pocket Books, 1965). All further page citations from this novel are from this edition and will be contained within parentheses in my text.

6. *Letters,* p. 38.

7. *Letters,* p. 38.

8. *Letters,* p. 12.

9. *Letters,* p. 54.

10. Floyd C. Watkins, "*Gone with the Wind* as Vulgar Literature," *Southern Literary Journal* 2 (Spring 1970), p. 97. See also Malcolm Cowley's review of *Gone with the Wind* in *New Republic* (Sept. 16, 1936), p. 161, and Belle Rosenbaum's "Why Do They Read It?" *Scribner's Magazine* 102 (Aug. 1937), p. 69.

11. Thomas Uzzell, "Mob Reading," *Saturday Review of Literature* 17 (Nov. 29, 1937), p. 18.

12. Judith Krantz, *Princess Daisy* (New York: Crown, 1980), p. 67.

13. Interestingly, even before the war, women are presented as adults and men as children. On p. 53 Mitchell describes Ellen as the real manager of Tara; Gerald simply takes all the credit for his wife's accomplishments.

14. Leslie Fiedler has cautioned me not to overlook Gerald's role here; it is father O'Hara who inculcates Scarlett with "land-love" and who provides Scarlett with a model in her desire to possess the land. Yet, interestingly, almost all of Gerald's references to the land involve an association of it with a maternal force; his desire for it is patterned on a desire for the mother.

15. In a letter to Harry Stillwell Edwards, Mitchell comments:

I wanted to picture in "Melanie" as in "Ellen" the true ladies of the old South, gentle and dear, frail in body perhaps, but never of courage, never swerving from what they believed the right path, and no matter what they were called upon to do, by rude circumstance, always remaining ladies." (*Letters,* p. 15)

16. Scarlett's train ride bears an obvious resemblance to that of Mitchell, returning home to her mother's deathbed.

17. Curiously, but appropriately, Scarlett imagines these women as having powers usually attributed to men. She thinks of Melanie as a "tower of strength," as a sword which "flash[es] between her and the world," and of her mother in much the same way.

18. David Willbern has pointed out to me that as the novel comes to its conclusion, descriptions of Rhett become more and more maternal. That is, in early chapters, the strength of Rhett's chest and back is emphasized; in later chapters, Rhett's waist thickens and his chest is perceived as "broad and

brown," to be used as "a cradle" or "a pillow." In other words, it closely resembles the protecting bosoms of Mammy or Dilcey.

19. Leslie A. Fiedler, *The Inadvertent Epic* (New York: Simon and Schuster, 1979), p.60.

20. Robert Gutwilling, "In History There's Never Been Anything Like It," *New York Times Book Review* (June 25, 1961), p. 6.

21. Marion J. Morton, " 'My Dear, I Don't Give a Damn': Scarlett O'Hara and the Great Depression," *Frontiers* 5, no. 3 (1981), p. 53.

22. Morton, p. 55.

23. Norman N. Holland, *The Dynamics of Literary Response* (New York: Norton, 1975), p. 27.

Forever Amber: "Swollen Up like a Stuffed Toad"

> Later, she and Nan examined [the gown] carefully, speculating. "It must be two-score years old, or more," said Nan. "I wonder who wore it last?"
> Amber shrugged. "His first wife, maybe. Or an old sweetheart. . . ."
> To her surprise she found when she put it on that it fitted her very well, almost as if it had been made for her.
> —Kathleen Winsor, *Forever Amber*

> Girls in our society have normally remained externally and internally in relationships with their preoedipal mother and have been preoccupied with issues of separation, identification without merging, mitigation of dependency, freedom from ambivalence. Girls cannot and do not "reject" their mother and women in favor of their father and men, but remain in a bisexual triangle throughout childhood and puberty.
> —Nancy Chodorow, *The Reproduction of Mothering*

October 16, 1944, was not only Kathleen Winsor's twenty-fifth birthday, but also the day she officiated over the public birth of her bestselling first novel, *Forever Amber*. Macmillan and Company opened its board room (dubbed "bawd room") for a tea to celebrate this double event and reviewers closed in on the beautiful young author. According to an account in the *Saturday Review of Literature*, one reporter "snipped a lock of the lady's hair to paste in his memory book" and another, gazing upon Winsor, was heard to sigh: "What a profile . . . and it goes all the way down."[1] The highlighting of such incidents in review articles at the expense of more serious consideration of Winsor's text really should come as no surprise; throughout elaborate publicity campaigns to promote sales of *Forever Amber*, Macmillan made every attempt to blur distinctions between Winsor and her book—thus, it was particularly appropriate that this novelist and her novel share birthdays. Reading prepublication advertisements and reviews one has difficulty distinguishing praise for the text from praise for its author. Richard Mealand, writing in *Publisher's Weekly*, for example, excuses himself for not having read the book but feels confident enough to comment on it, since he so obviously has read the author: "if the book is as good as the author is beautiful, then it looks as though Macmillan's have [*sic*] another *Gone with the Wind* on their hands."[2] And Macmillan knew how to push its product; where the novel appeared, Winsor appeared—if not in person, then in the form of an enlarged, glossy Reves-Belo photograph. The photo, a close-up of Winsor's face, graced the pages of numerous literary journals and prompted Bennett Cerf in the *Saturday Review* to comment: "The idea is to persuade the customer that when he [*sic*] buys a copy of a book, the lady who wrote it goes with it."[3]

Following publication, Macmillan did nothing to disentangle author from text. If anything, the situation became increasingly confused as Winsor was identified not only with her text, but also with its heroine. The portrait of Amber St. Clare on the novel's dust jacket certainly resembles the Reves-Belo photograph of Winsor: both women gaze somewhat petulantly at a viewer, head slightly turned, hair brushed back at the sides, neck encircled by a strand (or strands) of round beads. Periodicals quickly picked up on a possible author/heroine identification. In *Life*'s article on Winsor and her work we are told that Macmillan surely has a successful combination in its "beautiful new author" and her book about a "ravishingly beautiful" heroine.[4] The collapsing of author into heroine was a simple procedure, and one which was further encouraged by rumors, circulated even before Winsor sold the movie rights to her novel, that she would play Amber in the film version.

Certainly, the marketing of numerous novels, by both male and female authors, involves marketing an author's appearance, purposefully confusing an author's attractiveness with that of his or her book. And yet, given many comments on the proliferation of Winsor photographs as well as occasional male protests about this mode of bookselling, it is apparent that in marketing *Forever Amber*, Macmillan greatly expanded the possibilities of authorial involvement in book-selling. Further, given the enormous success of *Forever Amber*[5] it is apparent that this technique would undergo further expansion in the future. Despite objections raised by nonphotogenic male novelists such as Irving Stone ("Please don't think I begrudge the ladies their lovely looks, but I think someone should put the brakes on this cast-couching tendency among publishers"[6]), *Forever Amber* proved the profit in selling a book by its cover—a cover graced by the beautiful young female novelist or her equally beautiful female heroine.[7]

The marketing of *Forever Amber,* especially in paperback, did not end with its cover, however. If unimpressed by the figures of Amber St. Clare and Kathleen Winsor, a possible paperback buyer might be won over by sales figures, in both this country and abroad, for the hardcover book and film, all neatly summarized on the opening pages of Signet's paperback *Forever Amber.* A rhetorical question, "What accounts for this extraordinary appeal," following upon the sales summary, permits copywriters to promote Winsor's novel even further:

Most experts agree it's the magic combination of an unforgettable heroine, a breath-taking plot and the thrilling rendition of one of the most glamorous and tempestuous periods in history—Restoration England. Lest anyone think this is a simple task, it should be said here that the author spent thousands of hours in meticulous research and read 356 books in order to create an authentic background for the action.[8]

We must forego an undoubtedly fascinating probe into the identity of these "experts" in favor of conjectures about the 356 books read by Winsor. The claim itself is interesting. While it functions as an attempted validation of the history in this historical romance, it also promises a reader something familiar, a repetition of texts which have pleased in the past.[9] Although this sort of borrowing is not uncommon, Winsor engages in it with a vengeance. If Macmillan encourages a confusion of identity between author and heroine by making one imitate the other on covers of *Forever Amber,* Winsor complicates identity confusion within the text as she presents her heroine in scenes that mimic those of previous novels (the works of Ann Radcliffe, Defoe's *Moll Flanders* and *Journal of the Plague Year,* Mitchell's *Gone with the Wind* all come to mind).

But Macmillan's use of a derivative cover portrait and Winsor's use of derivative plot sequences really come nowhere near suggesting the magnitude of this novel's obsessive concern with personal derivations; cast in a mimic's role, heroine Amber unceasingly imitates female characters who have preceded her—characters from earlier texts as well as from the text which bears her name. Of course, this perpetual play of imitation leads to problems: who is Amber St. Clare? a thief? an actress? (the first two roles in which Winsor places her) a lady? does she actually have an identity of her own? The questions may seem simple—indeed adolescent—and so they should, because *Forever Amber* is a novel of adolescence, a novel that worries over issues (individuation and separation, ego-continuity, sexual identity) most often confronted by the adolescent female on her way to autonomous adulthood.[10] Further, as *Forever Amber* portrays the precarious nature of a female child's necessary turn from mother to father but continued emotional identification with her female parent, it addresses concerns articulated in recent feminist psychoanalytic considerations of female development.[11] It is the triangle of father/mother/daughter which shapes Winsor's text, just as it is Amber's regressive repetition of preoedipal and oedipal struggles which provides a pattern for Winsor's narrative.

This narrative stretches over 700 pages and traces ten years' worth of events in Amber's life. In Part I Winsor introduces a sixteen-year-old country wench; in Part VI she takes leave of a twenty-six-year-old courtesan. Curiously though, while Amber undoubtedly accrues a few wrinkles and most certainly improves her wardrobe over the years, she herself does not develop or grow in any significant way. Instead, she remains a confused sixteen-year-old, mimicking any available model as she attempts to construct an identity in reaction/relation to that of an imagined mother and father. Thus, the prevailing psychodynamic of this text might be described as psychostasis[12]—an inability to move beyond imitative adolescent behavior. The blurring of images on the cover of Macmillan's first edition of *Forever Amber* (author or heroine?) as well as the blurring of texts on the inside cover of Signet's paperback edition (356?), then, actually represent the text quite truthfully; on all levels, problems of autonomy and identity lead to a confusion between self and other, a tendency toward theft and imitation, and, finally, a debilitation associated with essential stasis.[13]

Sixteen years elapse between the end of Winsor's prologue and the first chapter of her novel. Amber St. Clare spends these years with her foster parents, Matthew and Sarah Goodegroome, in the small village of Marygreen. She knows virtually nothing about her real parents: John Mainwaring, undoubtedly lost in the Civil War, never returns to claim his fiancée and child; Judith Marsh lives only long enough to give life and a name to her newborn child. What Amber *does* know of her mother—a knowledge circumscribed by the boundaries of a small graveyard plot in Marygreen—leads her to associate the maternal line with a "narrow round of life," while what she does *not* know about her father allows her to associate him with the romance of life outside Marygreen, with stories of the Court told her by the local cobbler, with realms of infinite possibilities. Amber's preferred association of self with the male line finds reinforcement in the name given to her by her mother. After rejecting such matrilineal possibilities as "Judith," "Anne," or "Sarah," (after herself, her own mother, or the attending midwife, subsequently Amber's foster mother) Judith settles upon "Amber," the color of John Mainwaring's eyes. Thus, Amber St. Clare begins life with a pseudonymous surname selected by her father to conceal his true identity and a somewhat dubious "Christian" name, selected by her mother but based upon a look from the absent father's eyes. Both parts of this name reflect not only the precarious nature of its bearer's identity but also her dependence upon a father figure for identity confirmation.

In chapter one, Winsor supplies her heroine with a hero who might be her father. Like John Mainwaring, Bruce Carlton springs from a noble line, towers over other men, and possesses "strangely compelling eyes" (which elicit life-long devotion from sixteen-year-old females). The similarities between Carlton and Mainwaring may be wasted on Amber, but not on us. Of even more pronounced effect in yoking the two men together in a reader's mind is a statement made by Amber about Carlton's chief appeal: "She had never seen anyone like him before. . . . He was every handsome, gallant gentleman the cobbler had ever described."[14] Such is the appeal of a never-seen father as well.

Appropriately, every man of consequence in Amber's emotional life—and there are several in addition to Carlton—is stamped from precisely this same mold; Black Jack Mallard, Rex Morgan, and King Charles are all powerful, virile, over six feet tall, with square shoulders, lean hips, magnificent legs, and commanding eyes.[15] Of even more importance, each of these men, like an orphan's wished-for father, distinguishes Amber from other women, sets her apart, marks her as someone outside the mass of mothers and daughters. Carlton rescues Amber from a repetition of what she imagines her mother's Marygreen life to have been; Black Jack lifts her out of the squalor of a Newgate cell shared with other female offenders; Rex offers her a way out of the tiring room crowded with aspiring actresses; and Charles takes her from common chambers to install her in special Whitehall apartments. However, while this "distinguishing feature" attests to a father's power, it also must make us aware of the power of a mother, (or female other) from whom a daughter so desperately wants to distinguish herself. In *Forever Amber* Winsor insists upon the omnipotent maternal as she repeatedly depicts Amber in relation to men involved with women. From the first chapter of Part I to the final chapter of Part VI, Winsor's heroine doggedly directs her emotional energies to capturing the attention of a much-coveted male, but every such attempt propels Amber into some sort of relationship (mother, daughter, sister) with another female.[16] Thus, an understanding of Amber's relationship to mothers—surrogate and otherwise—is of equal if not greater importance than consideration of Amber's relationship to surrogate fathers. Following a course charted by Winsor, we might look first at female/female relationships triangulated by a male (daughter, mother, and father), then at female/female relationships in their own right.

Winsor begins with a series of scenes in which Amber, so as to capture the distinguishing, identity-confirming gaze of various men, first imitates, then surpasses, other women. For example, after meeting Bruce Carlton in Marygreen, Amber, to ensure a second meeting, must assume the manner and the costume of Meg, maid of the inn. Grabbing Meg's apron and several bottles of ale, Amber parades before Carlton and his men, eliciting a response which assures her that she is not perceived as a common barmaid. Once in London, Amber takes advantage of more numerous opportunities for modeling herself upon other women; she scrutinizes ladies of quality from the windows of her apartment, taking note of how they pick up their skirts, pull on their gloves, and use their fans, and when she attends the theater, she devotes more attention to the women in surrounding boxes than to the actors on stage. These hours of observation pay off not only in Amber's displays for Bruce but also, following his departure, in her performances for Black Jack Mallard, her next lover of any consequence. Amber attracts the attention of highwayman Black Jack while in Newgate, where she is detained for debt. After Jack helps her escape, she joins his household of thieves in Whitefriars, upsetting an earlier relationship between Jack and Bess Columbine. The latter, of Amber's approximate age, height, and coloring, regards the newcomer with jealous and angry eyes as Amber appropriates her position in the household. Although Amber disdains Bess as a slut of the vulgar, ill-bred variety, she apes her ways quite readily, quickly assuming not only Bess's place in Jack's bed, but her role in various hold-up schemes as well. Amber finds Bess's costume comfortable until she realizes that Jack, the final arbiter of taste, actually sees little difference between her style and that of Bess (he prefers Amber simply because she is a novelty). Clearly, Jack's nominal differentiation cannot provide Amber with a sense of self as distinct from Bess.

Similarly, after Amber escapes Whitefriars, takes to the stage, and steals her next lover from another actress, Beck Marshall, an issue of major importance is Amber's ability to distinguish herself from Beck. As at Whitefriars, Amber begins by following the other woman, moving into and finally appropriating her place in the tiring room, on stage, in Captain Rex Morgan's bed. Winsor suggests, however, that such appropriation may lead to the loss of personal boundaries; when Beck, furious with Amber, falls upon her, the two women, "clasped as tight as lovers," roll over and over, first one on top, then the other. Momentarily the two become one.

These episodes, however, really function only as prologue to the far more elaborate exploration of oedipal triangles occurring in Parts III and IV of the novel. In these central sections Winsor depicts Amber's marriages to Samuel Dangerfield and the Earl of Radclyffe, both old enough to be her father, both previously married to women of their own age, both with children older than Amber. The tension of these scenes derives primarily from the fluctuating nature of Amber's relationship to other women associated with Dangerfield and Radclyffe.

Amber meets and marries the former at Tunbridge Wells, where she retires temporarily following the death of Rex Morgan. A solidly established merchant, Dangerfield offers Amber a life of financial security. Along with this offer, however, comes the Dangerfield family: thirteen children and numerous grandchildren. As might be expected, these family members do not particularly welcome Amber as a new mother. Lettice, Dangerfield's oldest daughter, is most hostile. Twelve years older than Amber, Lettice resents this woman who now captures the gaze of her father, resents her most especially for her youthfulness and sexuality. When Amber, after several months of marriage, announces her pregnancy, Lettice takes the news as a serious shock, as a statement of her father's infidelity to her dead mother. Of course, Lettice's sense of her father's infidelity involves his infidelity to her as well. Amber is not unaware of her position relative to Lettice and the first Mrs. Dangerfield. Upon entering Dangerfield House she sees, in the drawing room, a portrait of Samuel and his first wife, another portrait in Samuel's apartments, as well as wardrobes and furniture, all of which bear the mark of the first Mrs. Dangerfield's personality. Amber decides immediately that the house must be redone to reflect her, rather than the first wife and her daughter (Lettice is almost an exact replica of her mother). Changing the maternal space, Amber completely dissociates herself from it, but also, she renders the dead mother yet more dead, which cannot help but anger the daughter who hopes to keep her alive. This daughter does not give up easily; maneuvering to regain her father's affections by discrediting Amber, Lettice discloses the fact that Amber once was an actress. Winsor traces the miserable failure of Lettice's attempt in an exchange of looks. As Lettice finishes her disclosure, Amber stares at her levelly, revealing all of the hatred she feels for her new stepdaughter; Samuel looks straight ahead (not at Lettice), then at Amber, who turns to him. The old husband and young wife gaze longingly at one another, then Samuel proudly takes Amber's arm and walks out of the room with her. Of importance here is the challenge exchanged between the two women (essentially, a declaration of war between mother and daughter) and the turn of both Samuel and Amber away from Lettice and toward each other. Amber's position as new mother is validated and then, a few chapters later, validated again as we learn of her pregnancy.

Having mined some of the tensions in a struggle between old mother and new from Amber's position as the latter, Winsor then shifts her focus: in the struggle between Amber and her fifteen-year-old step-daughter Jemima, Amber finds herself playing the role Lettice played in relation to her—now she is the older woman. Initially Amber and Jemima enjoy a friendship (Winsor's narrator notes that Amber usually likes the company of girls she considers too young or unattractive to compete with her). Jemima begins to imitate her stepmother's low necklines, painted lips, and black taffeta patches, an imitation sure to please a woman who herself delights in copying from others. However, when Jemima confides to Amber that she is in love with the handsomest man she has ever met and then announces that this marvelous man is Lord Bruce Carlton, the friendship immediately cools. Shocked, angry, and scared, Amber attempts to reassure herself; she reminds herself that Jemima is just a child, and a child nowhere near as attractive as Amber. But Amber cannot stop herself from scrutinizing Jemima's face, and wondering if this face poses "a threat to her own happiness" (p. 309). The moment is archetypal: declaring her affection for a man, a girl steps into the realm of women, and challenges the woman upon whom she has modeled herself. Amber studies the young woman she has helped to form: has she created a monster who will oust her from daddy's heart? Then too, Amber must study herself: have marriage and the assumption of maternal responsibilities rendered her less attractive? Winsor portrays the mutual scrutiny of step-mother and daughter in a scene that takes place immediately prior to Bruce Carlton's arrival at Dangerfield House for a formal supper. Jemima, still unaware of Amber's love for Bruce, bursts into her stepmother's bedroom, dressed in blue satin and looking prettier than Amber has ever seen her look. While wishing that Jemima might look more like Lettice, Amber turns away from the girl and dons a gown of champagne-colored lace over champagne satin. Jemima watches Amber as the latter, never returning Jemima's look, walks to a mirrored dressing-table and puts on her emeralds. Jemima cannot help but exclaim over Amber's beauty, and as she does so, she seeks her own reflection in the mirror, as if to reassure herself that Amber's radiance has not wholly blocked out her own. Refusing to meet Jemima's eyes, Amber bolsters her own sense of self as Jemima cannot take her eyes off her beautiful stepmother. Of course, with this tactic Amber also undermines Jemima's own sense of self, prompting the younger woman to seek reassurance in a mirror. Winsor's mirror play renders yet more fully the precarious nature of identity boundaries between mother and stepdaughter; looking for her own reflection, Jemima cannot avoid that of Amber. Even more perilous to Jemima than her inability to see herself separately from Amber is the possibility that while in Amber's company Bruce perhaps will not see Jemima at all; without the confirmation of his gaze she fears the loss not only of her reflection, but of her very self.

For a while, the ever-potent Bruce Carlton is able to make love to both mother and daughter, and to keep the affairs secret. During this time, Jemima comes to resemble Amber so closely as to be almost a parody of her; the two women dress, flirt, and make love alike. Apparently finding it difficult to avoid poking fun at these two, Winsor goes so far as to duplicate their conversational lines. For example, upon learning that Bruce is to set sail the following day, Amber rushes to his ships and pleads that he spare some time for her: "I had to see you again, Bruce, before you went" (p. 331). She is interrupted by a knock on the cabin door, and, hiding in an adjoining cabin, Amber listens as Jemima enters and addresses a similar plea to Bruce: "You're going away tomorrow! I've got to see you again!" (p. 332). The game is up and the mirroring of these two women comes to a climax when Jemima, who has found Amber's glove in Bruce's cabin, threatens to tell her father of his wife's infidelity; Amber then threatens to tell her husband of his daughter's premarital promiscuity. Enraged, Jemima hurls a newly learned insult; she calls Amber a whore. Never one to miss an opportunity, Amber returns the compliment. As if to finalize the collapse of boundaries between them, the women fall upon each other, slapping, scratching, and screaming (the scene repeats that between Amber and Beck Marshall). In addition to completing the psychological transgression noted earlier, imaged in Jemima's mirror scrutiny of self and mother, this scene of physical transgression also functions as further evidence of Amber's arrested development; never fully autonomous, she engages in a perpetual replay of adolescent battles.

While Amber's rather definitive retort ("you too are a whore") and the resulting battle may serve to cap off this example of female/female ambivalence, Winsor adds an epilogue: both Amber and Jemima are pregnant—and both by Bruce Carlton. Safely married, Amber may attribute the paternity of her child to Samuel; Jemima has no such alibi. Interestingly, Winsor here further complicates relations among women in her novel. As we read of Jemima's plight—pregnant by a man she loves but forced by her family to marry a man she detests— the plot line seems familiar. And well it should, since Winsor here repeats elements from her prologue, where she tells the story of Judith Marsh's love for John Mainwaring, her pregnancy by him, and her parents' insistence that she wed another man. In the prologue, it is Lady Anne Marsh, Judith's mother, Amber's grandmother, who opposes her daughter's desires most vehemently and who pressures her to wed Edmund Mortimer, Earl of Radclyffe. In Part III, Jemima's position resembles that of Judith, Amber's mother, while Amber's position duplicates that of Anne, her grandmother. Like Judith, Jemima pleads for permission to marry the man she loves, while Amber, like Anne, insists she will do no such thing, but will wed the spindly legged, pock-marked Joseph. Cuttle. Of importance in both scenes is preparation of the reluctant bride's wedding gown; both gowns are described in considerable detail (down to the last seed pearl), and it is during one of Jemima's fittings that Amber guesses her pregnancy, thereby gaining an advantage in this familial struggle. Finally, however, the stories diverge; Judith defied her mother and ran off with her lover, while Jemima, defeated by her stepmother, walks to the altar with young Cuttle.

This modified re-presentation of the Anne/Judith story is not gratuitous. On the contrary, in addition to supplementing an already large collection of mother/daughter stories, it reminds the reader of Amber's familial history and thus allows for a fuller understanding of the familial issues at play in Amber's next marriage. Following the death of Samuel, the birth of Amber's daughter Susanna, and the return, then departure of Bruce Carlton, Amber meets a debt-ridden "stinking old buck-fitch." She marries him because this buck-fitch comes with a title: he is Edmund Mortimer, Earl of Radclyffe. When Amber quizzes her friend Almsbury on the Earl's first impression of her, Almsbury reports the Earl as saying that Amber reminds him of someone, a lady, he knew a long time ago. This plot becomes more complicated when Amber and Radclyffe agree on a wedding day and he asks that rather than ordering a new gown, she wear one which he has laid away. Like Scarlett O'Hara and many other heroines of women's fiction, the uninquisitive Amber asks no questions as Radclyffe brings her a stiff white-satin gown, embroidered all over with tiny pearls, creased and slightly faded from having been packed for so many years. Nor does Amber experience any more than mild surprise when she discovers that the dress fits her very well, "almost as if it had been made for her" (p. 441).[17] Questions and exclamations belong to the reader, who soon realizes that yes, Radclyffe is the man who, years ago, was chosen by Amber's grandparents as suitable husband for their daughter. Thus, we come full circle, as daughter dons her mother's dress, weds her mother's betrothed, and assumes the title that was to have been hers. Only after eight rather miserable months of marriage does Amber ask Radclyffe about the previous owner of the dress, and he explains that she was a woman he intended to marry, but did not, a woman he sought, unsuccessfully, for twenty-three years and to whom he saw a resemblance in Amber. She experiences a moment of jealousy; angry that he once loved another woman, she lashes out at him.

Piqued at the thought of the other woman, Amber exacts her revenge, a double revenge. First, prior to Radclyffe's death she lures his son Philip into an adulterous, incestuous affair. The country-bred Philip is plagued with guilt; he loathes himself for having committed incest. Amber's response is completely opposite; she, no doubt like her author, delights in multiplying the triangular configurations in this family. Second, following Radclyffe's death, Amber sends for his papers, among which she discovers a letter apparently written by the woman Radclyffe had loved and sought so unsuccessfully for twenty-three years. She destroys the letter; momentarily having resurrected her mother for Radclyffe, Amber forces this other woman back into the grave, erases every sign of her.

When Winsor depicts Amber stepping into her mother's dress and into her son's (stepson's) bed she literalizes the replacement of mother by daughter, father by son. In a text preoccupied with the breakdown of personal identity constructs between mothers and daughters, it is not surprising that other familial/social constructs also show signs of strain. The most completely realized portrait of this potential for identity breakdown occurs in Amber's relationship to the woman Bruce Carlton finally chooses to wed. Arriving in London from one of his interminable trips abroad, Bruce teases Amber about her fourth marriage and then admits that he too has taken marital vows. Amber receives this news in stunned silence, feeling that the words of doom had been "between them always, inevitable as death" (p. 537). Winsor's rather trite simile is actually very appropriate here as it conveys the nature of a struggle to the death among three people. As the older woman in this triangle (Corinna, Bruce's wife, is about six years younger than Amber and close to eighteen years younger than Bruce), Amber wishes for the death of the woman who, structurally, enacts the role of daughter; repeatedly, she expresses her hatred of Corinna and her hope that Corinna might die. Amber quickly discovers, however, that in this instance it is the woman cast as mother who is rushed into an early grave. Bruce tells her that Corinna knows about their son, supposedly the product of an earlier marriage, and expects Bruce to bring back the boy with him when he returns to America. Immediately Amber asks what Bruce has told Corinna about the boy's mother, then stops, sickened, when she realizes that Bruce undoubtedly has rung the death knell for young Bruce's mother. Bruce admits that yes, he has done so. Thus one mother is dismissed so another may assume her place in relation to the father.

Hoping that her son's presence may keep Bruce's memory of her alive, Amber releases young Bruce to his father. Structurally, then, young Bruce repeats the relationship of his father to his mother: he goes away, explores new territories, while she waits for his occasional visits. Also, while young Bruce engages in his exploration, he may form other relationships with women of equal or greater importance to his relationship to Amber; she, however, remains caught in her relationship to him—and to any other woman he should introduce. Conveniently, having christened the child after his father, Winsor doubles the possibilities of triangular conflict: the battle for father Bruce is reflected in the battle for son Bruce. So, for example, when Amber relinquishes young Bruce to his father, she tries to push all thought of Corinna from her mind; she cannot tolerate the thought "of another woman's having him" (p. 562). Of course, the "him" in this case refers to her male child, but it easily may be applied to the father of this child as well.

Amber's desire to be recognized as someone other than/someone different from the woman with whom she must share her lover and her son finds expression not only in her wish that Corinna might come to an early death, but also in Amber's attempts to upstage Corinna publicly, to take all eyes away from this newcomer. Learning that Lady Carlton is to be introduced to London society on a Thursday evening at Arlington House and knowing that if the Lady be even moderately pretty she will attract all eyes, Amber determines to put on the show of her life. She calls in her dressmaker and instructs her to make a gown different from anything seen before, a gown guaranteed to take the crowd's attention away from Corinna. As Amber models the nearly transparent black gown, her dressmaker assures her that with Amber in the room, no one will even look at "the other one." Amber arrives at Arlington House, is announced and, sure enough, every eye turns toward her. As she enters, heads turn, eyes bulge, and "even King Charles turned on his heel . . . and stared" (p. 649). Horrified at her mistake, Amber passionately wishes that she were home "where no one could see her": in other words, she wishes to enact the annihilation she experiences in the eyes of this crowd. Instead, Amber must remain and watch the entrance of Lord and Lady Carlton: the latter, beautiful, young, and discreetly dressed, captures the looks of approval Amber desired.

Amber's precarious sense of identity is subject to yet another trial later in the evening, when she retires to the ladies' dressing room. Staring at her own reflection in a mirror, she sees Corinna: the younger woman stands in the doorway. Staging here duplicates that of the scene discussed earlier between Amber and Jemima; now, as then, the moment is fraught with tension; two women in love with the same man look into the mirrored reflection of each others' eyes and wonder how they are to distinguish one from the other.

Not long after, Amber pays a private call on Corinna and learns that Corinna and Bruce will not be sailing for France as early as planned because Corinna is with child. Stunned, Amber again perceives a threat to her position as mother of Bruce's children. Taking leave of Corinna, then, Amber cannot help but make an attempt to salvage something of her own role. As she walks out the doorway, she comments that she met Corinna's son yesterday at the Palace. The line is, of course, merely a ploy; Amber wants to hear a denial of maternity from Corinna's own lips. Corinna obliges, but adds that she loves the boy "as if he were my own." The claim to affectional possession further enrages Amber, who suggests that she would have thought Corinna might hate her husband's first wife and everything associated with her. Corinna responds rather ingenuously, asking why she should hate the first wife when "he belongs to me now" (p. 667). At this point, Winsor's narrator clarifies by pointing out that Corinna refers to the father, not the son. As in earlier instances, Corinna may well be speaking of either; differentiation between the two males is of far less importance and is far less problematic than differentiation between the two females.

Winsor repeats the dynamics of female convergence in a final scene between Amber and Corinna. Unable to find Bruce and be reconciled with him before he sets sail for France, Amber calls upon his wife. The two women stare at each other, delving into each other's eyes: "mortal enemies, two women in love with the same man" (p. 712). Curiously, although the emotion exchanged here is one of intense hatred, the fact of its intensity and of its exchange brings the two women together. Amber breaks the look and asserts herself by taunting the other woman with the fact that finally everything Lord Carlton has will devolve to Amber's son, rather than to any child produced by Corinna. Possessive pronouns (your, my) are of utmost importance in Amber's speech, as she uses her male child to substantiate her claims to the father and to her own unique identity. And yet, the possibility of falling into the other woman, of losing one's self, is ever present. Immediately after Amber declares her superiority as mother, hierarchical boundaries grow hazy once again. Almost like lovers, the two women stand transfixed, "breathing each other's breath" (p. 714). For a moment, they engage in a mutual self-hypnosis; each both finds and loses herself in the eyes of the other. They really only awaken at the sound of Bruce's voice. Furious with Amber, he shouts her name, strides toward her, strikes her. With this slap, all of the anger, all of the ambivalence that Amber has felt toward Corinna transfers itself to Bruce; she returns blow for blow as the hatred she has harbored for Corinna wells up and out of her. Of interest here is the way in which Amber explodes boundaries of emotion (love/hate) and object (Corinna/Bruce); her rage resembles that of a young girl, furious with the two human beings she loves most: mother and father. Triumphantly, Corinna now assumes the function of a mother, splitting the two combatants, looking upon Bruce "with a pity that was almost maternal" (p. 715) and claiming his attention with a mother's plea: "Bruce—I think you must send for the midwife. The pains come often now—" (p. 715). So, in this final round between Corinna and Amber, Corinna plays a trump card (her belly) and wins the further affections of father.

Although Corinna triumphs in this exchange between Amber and herself as she presents dramatic evidence of her maternal qualifications, maternity does not always take the prize. Rather, both in this scene and in numerous others, maternity is approached with trepidation, with an awareness of its doubleness. While the maternal role allows for a far greater claim on the affections of father, it also allows for the collapse of self into one's mother and the metamorphosis of one's body into something alien, something other. If identity boundaries are problematic for the female child, problems arise once again when the adult female bears a child. As the child has difficulty differentiating self from other, so too the mother who, for nine months, not only encompasses this other being but also loses control over the body she formerly identified as self.[18] Winsor most fully conveys dangers of the maternal position in a second cluster of scenes which, like those discussed above, give a definite structure to the novel as they present and re-present a configuration of characters—this time, exclusively female characters caught in an exclusively female space: the body that may give birth.

We need not read far for the first of these scenes, as Winsor sets the prologue of her novel in a lying-in chamber. Her opening sentence, describing the chamber, obviously suggests a female space: "The small room was warm and moist" (p. 7). As Winsor continues her description of the room and of the various women who occupy it, the space becomes increasingly ominous. A midwife works with her hands on the woman who just has given birth, and various village wives watch with "tense anxious faces." The woman who has given birth, Judith Marsh, slips into a reverie but awakens to cramps and pain—which do not abate. Raising her hand, Judith notes that it is smeared with blood. Only then do we understand, as Judith understands, the source of the chamber's tension and the meaning of its signs: in the process of giving birth, Judith's body betrays her. She turns frantically to the midwife, pleading for help, insisting that she does not want to die, but the midwife Sarah cannot stop the blood which flows between Judith's legs. Who could ask for more in an opening chapter? Winsor rivals Margaret Mitchell in her ability to convey the horrors of a confinement chamber, horrors stemming in large part from the pregnant woman's sense of confinement within her own body. Perhaps Winsor even surpasses Mitchell. When the barely pregnant Melanie Wilkes retreats into her narrow bedroom to die, she takes her unborn child with her. Judith dies only after experiencing what she perceives as a final betrayal on the part of her body; with unmistakable disappointment she learns she has given birth to a daughter rather than a son.

Of course, it is easy to read this mother's death as the first casualty in the ongoing struggle between mothers and daughters which *Forever Amber* documents, but of equal importance, surely, is an understanding of this death as first instance of a woman taken prisoner by her own body. This language is not too strong, as the text shows only a few chapters later, when the sixteen-year-old daughter of Judith learns that she too is to become a mother. At first the knowledge does not burden Amber, as she hopes thus to convince the sea-faring Bruce to remain in London with her. But Bruce, as usual, abandons her for his ship, and as weeks pass Amber feels increasingly frightened by the realization that "imprisoned within her body, growing with each day that passed, was proof of her guiltiness" (p. 85); Amber here figures her body as prison, the embryo as prisoner. Not long after, she refines this imagery. Riding back from the Royal Exchange, Amber and her new acquaintance Mrs. Sally Goodman witness the public whipping of a woman who has given birth to a bastard child. Amber cries out in horror as the whip slashes across this convict's shoulders, but Sally tells her not to waste her sympathy on such a wretched creature who undoubtedly deserves the punishment she receives. Amber, who identifies wholeheartedly with this mother, cannot help but sympathize; in a frenzy, she reminds herself that all too soon *she* will be in that convict's shoes. The prisoner-mother functions as possible model for all mothers—and Amber is not far off in her prediction that she herself will follow this woman's steps. Without a husband, Amber experiences her pregnancy "closing in on her," shutting her into "a room from which there was no escape" (p. 97). Terrified of this imagined room, Amber accepts the marriage proposal of Sally's so-called nephew Luke Channell. When Luke and Sally cheat her of her money and make her responsible for their numerous bills, however, the pregnant Amber finds herself shut into a literal room; she is taken to Newgate for debt. With three other entering prisoners, Amber must await cell assignment in the Condemned Hold. A description of this room opens chapter nine; the floor is covered with sour-smelling rushes, and the stone walls are "moist and dripping and green with a mossy slime" (p. 105). Placing this description at the beginning of the chapter and insisting on details which generate a sense of constriction as well as an atmosphere of dread, Winsor links the Condemned Hold to the lying-in chamber of her prologue; these spaces—and the space of the maternal body—resemble each other in curious, ominous ways.

If the lying-in chamber of the prologue serves as prototype for the Newgate hold of chapter nine, Moll Turner, a "morose slattern" chained to the wall across from Amber, serves as possible prototype for the pregnant, first-time offender. Two other women, a young Quaker and a middle-aged housewife, also sit chained in the hold, but it is to the "dirty slut with large open sores on her face and breasts" that Amber directs her inquiries about the prison. As Moll Turner answers Amber's questions and interjects anecdotes from her own life, Winsor suggests various affinities between the two superficially dissimilar females.[19] Upon learning that Amber is pregnant and cannot call upon her family, Moll nods knowingly. She explains that she too began by getting pregnant, pregnant by a handsome captain in the King's army. When her father expressed his disapproval, Moll ran off. Like Amber, and like Amber's mother Judith, this woman escapes her family for a man, only to find herself caught in another, no less confining net. Winsor spells out the connection to be drawn as she describes Amber staring at Moll with fascinated horror; the new convict does not want to believe that "this ugly emaciated sick creature had once been young and in love with a handsome man, *just as she was*" (p. 109; my italics). While Amber sees herself, years hence, in Moll, Winsor adds one final bit of information about the latter, further enhancing the reflective possibilities of this mirror: Moll is thirty-two. This fact is insignificant until we add Amber's age (sixteen) to that of her mother at her death (sixteen-seventeen) and realize that Moll's birthdate must fall somewhere in the same year as Judith's; if the latter had lived, would she resemble her contemporary? In the process of becoming a mother herself, can Amber avoid becoming like either of these two mothers (one dead, the other nearly so)?

Of more immediate concern to Amber than Moll's metamorphic decay from pleasing young woman to repellent old hag is the physical metamorphosis wrought on her own body by pregnancy. Winsor is no less concerned; while her description of Judith's ordeal during delivery may provoke sympathy and fear on the part of a female reader, her minutely detailed presentation of Amber, seven months' pregnant, must call forth feelings of revulsion and lead to serious questions about the desirability of motherhood. Winsor notes the numerous "sad changes" wrought on Amber's appearance: she no longer can button her bodice and her skirt hangs inches shorter in front; her gown is stained with perspiration and spotted with food; her stockings are streaked with runs and her shoes are scuffed; her teeth are slick with film, her hair is snarled with grease, and her face is grimy with dirt. Eerily, the look of 'fascinated horror' that Amber directed at old mother Moll Turner, we now direct at her, the mother-to-be. Of course, one might argue that under ordinary circumstances pregnancy is not quite so miserable; after all, grease and dirt collect in Amber's hair not because she is pregnant but because she is in prison. But the text overrides this argument as it insists that maternity itself is a prison, a "growing, living net," a small room from which escape is possible only after nine months.

After Amber leaves Newgate and gives birth to her child she undergoes several more pregnancies. Although none of these is reported in as much detail as her first, Amber never fails to protest against this unwanted and apparently unlimitable change in her body/herself. At times her protest takes the form of a sharp admonition to the maid to lace her more tightly, to hold her burgeoning waist in as far as possible; at other times, so upset with the prospect of being "misshapen," Amber terminates the pregnancy early, with an abortifacient. Winsor's most alarming example of pregnancy as a "looming monster" (p. 94), however, occurs not in reference to one of Amber's bouts with maternity, but rather, to that of numerous anonymous women, pregnant during the Great London Fire. As Amber rides into the burning city, one of the sights to greet her, amid clouds of smoke and crowds of people, is that of pregnant women:

There were a great many women, desperately trying to protect their awkward bellies, and several of the younger ones were crying, almost hysterical with terror. . . . A woman lying in a cart rolled slowly by; she was groaning and her face was contorted in the agony of childbirth; beside her knelt a midwife, working with her hands beneath the blankets, while the woman in her pain kept trying to throw them off. (P. 492)

Once more, Winsor uses setting as commentary on maternal situations; to be caught in the raging fire would seem to pose no more of a threat to these beings than to be caught in their expanding bodies. Also, once more, Winsor is unable to take her eyes off these terrified women; while touching on other members of the populace cursorily, she grants extended attention only to women with bulging bellies. Quite obviously, this author shares her heroine's ambivalence about the maternal body. Stripped to its essentials, the scene above works in the same way as Margaret Mitchell's famous Atlanta fire scene, discussed in the previous chapter. In both, a heroine must cope with the incessant demands of other female bodies, trying to bring babies into a world that falls apart on all sides. Upon confrontation with the female body Scarlett and Amber experience feelings of helplessness, desperation, and betrayal—feelings that stem from a fear that like the women before their eyes, they too may fall apart, may lose boundary integrity.

In 1944, *Forever Amber* finished fourth on the list of best-selling fiction; by 1945 it had moved to the top. What constituted the appeal of Winsor's novel? Of course, Macmillan and Winsor waged an extensive marketing campaign on behalf of the novel; they promised prospective buyers a bawdy Restoration setting and a "happy harlot" heroine. *Forever Amber* only half-fulfills these promises, however; curiously, it is precisely where the novel defaults that it most succeeds. First, despite the 356 historical texts read by Winsor while preparing her work, *Forever Amber,* like the majority of historical novels, is not true to its chosen period; although Amber dons seventeenth-century dress, she wears this dress according to twentieth-century dictates—with specific reference to the 1940's in America. Winsor suggests as much in an offhand response to charges of sexual daring in *Forever Amber:* "If anything, what I write is an understatement compared to the goings-on as I *hear* about them."[20] During the five years she devoted to *Forever Amber* (1939 to 1944), Winsor was not *hearing* about the Duke of Buckingham's excesses or King Charles's newest mistresses or the latest in Whitehall scandals; she was hearing about much more contemporary "goings-on," quite probably from women who, like herself, were awaiting the return of a male from overseas.[21] Thus, we might look to Winsor's heroine for clues about anxieties and fantasies engaging American women left behind as husbands, lovers, brothers, and sons fought the war over the seas. These women, like Amber, assumed the psychic responsibilities of "keeping the home fires burning." While doing so they channeled their energies into conduits previously closed and began to see themselves, and one another, in wholly new ways. Then, of course, the men returned, and these women once again were expected to regear, to shift back to earlier emotional structures—very much like Amber upon every return of Bruce Carlton.[22]

The novel does not fully live up to its advertised "Restoration authenticity" (and what novel could?); nor does it actually provide its readers with a happy harlot heroine. Since the success of *Moll Flanders,* booksellers and reviewers most often have assumed a very simple, positive relationship between the harlot heroine and her female readers. William Du Bois, writing in *New York Times Book Review,* operates on this assumption when he predicts that *Forever Amber,* with its feisty heroine, "is a booksellers' natural" because "few characters in fiction are more beloved by female readers than the successful harlot."[23] Du Bois to the contrary, Amber is *not* a successful harlot. Yes, she progresses from Marygreen to Whitechapel, from country wench to King's mistress, but she never gets what she wants: Bruce Carlton. She may hold him temporarily (as when she nurses him during the plague and comforts herself with the thought that no matter how often he has left her in the past, she possesses him fully during his sickness and convalescence), but Bruce always extricates himself, leaving Amber with empty arms. Winsor presents Amber's failure most clearly in a short but definitive exchange between heroine and hero. After pushing Bruce to admit that he loves her, Amber asks why Bruce won't marry her. He responds that love has nothing to do with his marriage. Amber then protests that love has everything to do with it, that the two of them no longer are children who must obey parents, but are adults who may do as they please. Bruce is right, however; love has nothing to do with his refusal to marry Amber. He refuses because a marriage between these two would violate the oedipal fantasy which *Forever Amber* allows its readers to indulge.[24] Essentially, in *Amber* readers find a heroine who acts out desires they experience, but repress; with Amber these readers may wage war on mother, frolic with father—and do so *safely,* because Amber never succeeds in making this frolic official. Further, readers may enjoy Amber's disappointment on the marriage market; obviously, since Amber "suffers for her sins" it is Amber—and not a reader—who must be guilty of oedipal desires.

Thus, *Forever Amber* offers its female readers pleasure without guilt, experience without the repercussions of experience. This marvelously conservative economy of fantasy (which is very much in keeping with the novel's social conservatism since you do not really want to be a happy harlot; better you should be grateful for your stodgy but reliable husband and two tiresome children) guarantees that Winsor's novel will be—in the words of William Du Bois— "a booksellers' natural."

Notes

1. Bennett Cerf, "Trade Winds," *Saturday Review of Literature* 27 (Nov. 4, 1944), p. 18.

2. Richard Mealand, "Books into Film," *Publishers' Weekly* (Sept. 16, 1944), p. 999.

3. Cerf, p. 18.

4. *Life,* 17 (Oct. 30, 1944), pp. 41-44.

5. According to figures in *Eighty Years of Bestsellers* by Alice Payne Hackett and James Henry Burke (New York: R. R. Bowker, 1977), the combined total for hardcover and paperback sales of *Forever Amber* as of 1975 was 2,925,268 (p. 14).

6. Quoted by Cerf, p. 18.

7. The cover of Signet's 1954 paperback is interesting as well. Winsor's name is placed directly opposite a portrait of Amber; confusion between the two is easily understandable, given the designer's obvious intention of associating novelist's name with heroine's face.

8. Publicity blurb on the inside cover of Signet's thirteenth printing in paperback of Kathleen Winsor's *Forever Amber* (no date).

9. Booksellers in the 1970's and 1980's promote lines of books with this tactic. Knowing that their audience wants a particular formula, they guarantee that this formula will be fulfilled on the basis of a particular cover design or logo.

10. I use the word "autonomy" as it is defined by Ellen Rothchild, "Female Power: Lines to Development of Antonomy," in *Female Adolescent Development,* ed. Max Sugar (New York: Brunner/Mazel, 1979), p. 275: "autonomy connotes sufficient psychologic separation from others so that one can assume responsibility for the self and can choose and initiate action in accord with one's own independently set guidelines; ideally we expect this by the end of adolescence."

11. See, for example, Nancy Chodorow's *The Reproduction of Mothering* (Berkeley: University of California Press, 1979).

12. I owe this term to Mary Childers, who, along with other members of a SUNY-Buffalo Women's Writing Group, saw this chapter in rough draft and generously offered suggestions for revision.

13. Of interest here is the fact that unlike *Gone with the Wind,* the bestseller to which it so often is compared, *Forever Amber* has not maintained an audience over the years. Although paperback editions of the novel were reissued during the 1950's, it currently is out of print.

14. Kathleen Winsor, *Forever Amber* (New York: Signet, thirteenth printing), p. 27. All further page citations from this text are from this edition and will be included in parentheses within the chapter.

15. We've seen this hero before (think of Rhett Butler) and will see him again (Mike Rossi in *Peyton Place,* Lyon Burke in *Valley of the Dolls,* Vito Orsini in *Scruples*). This apparently stock figure plays daddy for a wide range of little girls.

16. See Chodorow, p. 121.

17. A somewhat similar scene occurs in Daphne du Maurier's 1938 bestseller, *Rebecca* (New York: Doubleday, 1938), pp. 198-202, when Maxim de Winter's second wife dons a costume which duplicates that worn by his first wife, Rebecca: "Why the dress, you poor dear, the picture you copied of the girl in the gallery. It was what Rebecca did at the last fancy dress ball at Manderley. Identical. The same picture, the same dress" (p. 202).

18. Winsor does not depict earlier body transformations in Amber's life: the onset of menstruation, breast development, and so on. Contemporary analysts, however, are quick to discuss identification problems attendant upon

these transformations—problems similar to those which attend the move into motherhood (cf. Maj-Britt Rosenbaum, "The Changing Body Image of the Adolescent Girl," in *Female Adolescent Development,* ed. Max Sugar [New York: Brunner/Mazel, 1979]).

19. Given Moll's name and the setting in which Moll and Amber meet, there is a suggestion of affinities to yet a third female: Daniel Defoe's Moll Flanders. Surely one of the 356 books read by Winsor was *Moll,* a novel about a woman who "was Born in Newgate . . . was Twelve Years a Whore, Five Times a Wife," etc. Connections to Amber are obvious.

20. Quoted in "Kathleen Winsor," *Contemporary Authors Vols. 97–100,* ed. Frances Locher (Detroit: Gale Research Co., 1981), p. 569; my italics.

21. Winsor's own husband, Lt. Robert John Herwig, was with the Marines in the South Pacific. A photo on p. 44 of *Life's* portrait of Winsor shows her writing a "daily letter" to her man in uniform (she divorced Herwig in 1946 and then, like Amber, set off on a course of subsequent marriages and divorces).

22. Mary P. Ryan, in *Womanhood in America: From Colonial Times to the Present* (New York: New Viewpoints, 1979), p. 190, notes:

Two months after the end of World War II, 800,000 women had been fired by aircraft companies. International Business Machines immediately reactivated its policy against hiring married women. By 1947 women had practically disappeared from the heavy industries where they had received nearly man-sized wages during the war. The employment of women by automotive companies was reduced from 25 to 7.5 percent of their labor force, and the remaining female employees were largely in low-paying clerical positions. By November 1946, more than 2 million women had been summarily dismissed from their jobs and most of them were seeking new employment opportunities.

23. William Du Bois, "Jumbo Romance of Restoration London," *New York Times Book Review* (Oct. 15, 1944), p. 7.

24. David Cowart, in "Oedipal Dynamics in *Jane Eyre,*" *Literature and Psychology* 31, no. 1 (1981), p. 36, describes a very similar process of fantasy management. He explains that upon reading of the initial betrothal of Jane to Mr. Rochester, he experiences feelings of anxiety. He then goes on to explain the source of these feelings:

My disquiet, I believed, stemmed from a sudden alienation at the fantasy level. The oedipal core-fantasy of the novel is enjoyable as long as it is not susceptible of gratification, but when the fantasy is to be fulfilled, when the child will possess the parent, certain mature inhibitions—chiefly the incest taboo—come into play and expose one to primal anxiety and guilt.

Similarly, we may enjoy Amber's escapades with Bruce as long as they remain simple escapades—as long as they are not "susceptible of gratification."

— 3 —

Peyton Place: "The Uses—and Abuses—of Enchantment"

I could tell you some stories, honey, that ain't nothin' like the stories you tell me.
> —Grace Metalious, *Peyton Place*[1]

[Fairy tales] in a much deeper sense than any other reading material, start where the child really is in his [*sic*] psychological and emotional being. They speak about his severe inner pressures in a way that the child unconsciously understands, and without belittling the most serious inner struggles which growing up entails—offer examples of both temporary and permanent solutions to pressing difficulties.
> —Bruno Bettelheim, *The Uses of Enchantment*

A photograph on the back cover of Dell's twenty-fifth printing of *Peyton Place* shows author Grace Metalious seated in front of her typewriter, surrounded by the props of her trade: a cigarette burns in the glass ashtray and a pile of manila envelopes (containing manuscript, of course) litters the table. This representation of the "young author at work," however, differs slightly from others of its kind; rather than book-lined shelves behind Metalious's head we find brightly printed kitchen curtains; rather than a regulation-size desk for Metalious's typewriter we find a converted kitchen table. Just to be sure that we do not miss the message of the photograph, marketers at Dell provide an explanatory blurb: "Grace Metalious is the young housewife in blue jeans who created America's most controversial novel." In other words, Metalious is a "housewife-novelist": because of the latter term, she sits at a typewriter; because of the former, she sits at a typewriter in the kitchen. Of course, Metalious is not only a housewife-novelist, she is *the* housewife-novelist who created *Peyton Place*, a phenomenal best-seller.[2] As such, she may be marketed by Dell as the embodiment of a peculiarly twentieth-century female fantasy: while remaining at home, a woman might engage in imaginative musings, write a famous book, and become a celebrity. Having been kissed by an advertising agent, she becomes a twentieth-century Cinderella.[3] Such is the lure with which Dell attracts its housewife audience: Grace did it, and so can you.

Ironically, Dell could not have hit upon a sales pitch more in keeping with the thematic concerns and formal tensions of Metalious's work. While employing formal techniques of fairy tale (repetition, splitting and doubling of characters, exaggeration and overdetermination of incident, systematic distribution of rewards and punishments), while suggesting fairy tale analogues for her heroine (Sleeping Beauty, Snow White, Beauty of Beauty and the Beast), Metalious exposes the debilitating limitations of this genre as a fantasy form for women.[4] Certainly, Metalious encourages our identification with her heroine Allison (like us, a reader of fairy tales), but she also urges a critical distance from a heroine who too easily identifies herself with fairy tale fantasies. Unlike Dell publicity agents who blur distinctions between writer and reader, reader and text, unlike advertisers for Harlequin books who propose that women "disappear" into romances they read,[5] Metalious, in *Peyton Place*, actually promotes a policy of critical evaluation and assertive individuation in the face of fantasy. As she comments upon her text, as she raises questions about its very form, Metalious distinguishes *Peyton Place* from those "ostensibly innocuous fantasies . . . which glorify passivity, dependency, and self sacrifice as a heroine's cardinal virtue."[6] In the following pages, I am interested first in detailing Metalious's use of fairy tale forms as structure for a twentieth-century women's best-seller, and second, in analyzing her critique of these forms as structure for twentieth-century women's experience.

Written by a woman, for an audience comprised primarily of women, *Peyton Place* focuses on the story of a woman; in it, we follow the passage of a young girl from childhood to adolescence to womanhood. Early critics and reviewers of the novel note that this is not the story of one woman—rather, we read about the lives of three: Allison, Constance, and Selena.[7] Yet clearly, Metalious forefronts Allison, encourages reader identification with her, and employs the other two as alternatives, as options against which a reader may gauge the heroine's progress in her passage to womanhood. Thus, as in fairy tale—or, more accurately, as in fairy tale collections—the reader of *Peyton Place* is presented with a single story (a young girl's confrontation and resolution of ambivalence directed toward her mother, father, and love object) told over and over again, in slightly different guise, with slightly different emphases.[8] Of course, it is precisely these differences in the midst of similarity which both prompt and allow a critical evaluation of Allison's choice of plot permutation—and suggest a choice for us, as readers.

After an introductory chapter in which she maps the geography of Peyton Place, Metalious introduces her heroine, Allison MacKenzie. Watching a crowd of children leave the schoolyard on a Friday afternoon, Miss Elsie Thornton, eighth-grade teacher, notes "one child who walked alone. This was Allison MacKenzie, who broke away from the throng as soon as she reached the pavement and hurried down Maple Street by herself" (p. 14). Although Miss Thornton quickly shifts her attention to others among the schoolchildren (thereby providing a thumbnail sketch of this novel's cast of younger characters), her demarcation of Allison as the "peculiar child," the "child who walks alone," sets Allison apart for a reader; this character deserves special attention; this character may reflect a reader's own occasional feelings of peculiarity. Metalious reinforces this demarcation in chapter three, where she follows Allison to "Road's End," a private place at the end of town, to which Allison retreats when she needs to indulge her desires to "be by herself and to think her own thoughts." External characteristics of Allison's escape environment easily translate into characteristics of the internal environment of a reader engaged in "escape fiction." Such a reader positions herself, mentally, at "Road's End," away from the demands of others, away from the clamor of "everyday life."[9] Allison knows that she does not fit in: she prefers pleasures that others consider "babyish," admits she has a "headful of silly dreams," and fears graduation into high school, where she will be ridiculed as "the only odd and different member of the population" (p. 20). Clearly, we are to sympathize and identify with the young girl who is so obviously more sensitive than other characters around her. Another, more subtle, push for reader/heroine identification occurs as a result of authorial reticence; we receive no specific physical description of Allison. When Miss Thornton looks at the thirteen-year-old, she sees a child "still plump with residual babyhood, her eyes wide open, guileless and questioning; above that painfully sensitive mouth" (p. 14): all generalized, nonrestrictive attributes. We do not know the color of Allison's hair or eyes, the shape of her head, or her basic body build; any one of us might resemble her.

A third, even more important way in which Metalious prompts reader identification with Allison is by turning Allison herself into a reader. Metalious notes, several times, Allison's preoccupation with stories. The first such notation (which informs all subsequent ones) occurs in an exchange between Allison and her mother. The latter, coming home to find her daughter reading a book, asks what appears to be an oft-repeated question: "What are you reading now?" (p. 30). Allison replies: "Just a babyish fairy tale . . . I like to read them over once in a while. This one is The Sleeping Beauty" (p. 30). Metalious's choice of fairy tale text could not be more appropriate for Allison who, dissatisfied with her present reality, finds, via fairy tale, the possibility of another reality, and for us, who, reading *Peyton Place*, follow the progress of a Sleeping Beauty heroine as we steep ourselves in a modern day version of fairy tale wish fulfillment. Metalious's choice of text also, however, serves as warning; when Allison finishes her book, she falls asleep, reenacting the fate of Sleeping Beauty; as readers, we must beware of falling victim to the same fate.

Allison duplicates the nonactivity of her chosen fairy tale heroine at the end of chapter four, but unlike the slumbering princess, Allison must wake the following morning to confront problems of impinging adolescence. It is here that issues addressed covertly in traditional fairy tale are introduced overtly in the novel. A quick survey of any fairy tale collection furnishes repeated examples of stories set precisely at the moment the hero/heroine moves from childhood into adulthood. The move is represented in physical or situational change and prompts intense ambivalence between parent and child.[10] Interestingly, while Allison admits to certain physical changes, she would prefer to remain in a static "babyish world," a world that would not force her into the body of a woman, a body capable of being a mother and of assuming the role of her own mother. It is in her attitude toward menstruation, an obvious sign of womanhood, that Allison most emphatically expresses her ambivalence. She determines that periods may afflict other girls, but not her: "She decided that she would never tolerate such things in herself . . . 'I'll be the only woman in the whole world who won't, and I'll be written up in all the medical books' " (p. 73)—in other words, she will *be* the Sleeping Beauty, the figure for whom time stops. In avoiding menstruation, Allison hopes to distinguish herself from the crowd, to merit the status of princess in a world of commoners. Allison's determination, however, does not stop biology. When she wakes on the morning of her thirteenth birthday to discover blood, she is "disappointed, disgusted, and more than a little frightened" (p. 73). As Metalious explains, however, the reason Allison weeps is that "she was not, after all, going to be as unique as she had wanted to be" (p. 73). Several items are worthy of note here. First, Allison's understanding of the significance of her menstrual period corresponds to the significance of female puberty in numerous fairy tales. It is the time at which young girls must be put to sleep, locked in towers, or abandoned in forests, because, suddenly, they are capable of being sexually threatened by men *and* of posing sexual threats to women. Kay Stone, in a recent feminist analysis of fairy tales, observes that heroines such as Rapunzel, Snow White, and Sleeping Beauty all have their freedom severely curtailed at puberty, "a time in life when heroes are discovering full independence and increased power . . . this restriction [on women] reflects anxiety about competition with other women that increased sexuality offers."[11] Second, although one might accuse Metalious of contrivance in conflating menstrual and birthday rituals (and thirteen is such a perfect, magical number), she merely follows the convention of fairy tale, where rituals gain their full force precisely because they are contrived and consciously overdetermined. Further, the conflation is an economic one, as it allows Metalious an opportunity to depict Allison's first exposure to adolescent sexuality as well; at her birthday party, Rodney Harrington pulls Allison to him and "press[es] his mouth against hers" (p. 78).

Allison's confusion is not confined to the perimeters of her own body, however; it includes the woman whose body most resembles her own, whose body gave her birth: Constance MacKenzie. As Allison enters adolescence, the relationship between mother and daughter becomes especially problematic for both females. On the evening mentioned previously, after Allison puts down "Sleeping Beauty," gazes at a photograph of her father, and prepares for bed, she allows her mind to entertain thoughts of her mother's death: "For a moment she wondered what her life might have been like if it had been her mother who had died and her father who had lived. At once, she sank her teeth into the edge of the bed sheet in shame at this disloyal thought" (p. 32). For one unrestrained moment, Allison indulges in a standard oedipal fantasy (to be daddy's little girl, his *only* little girl) and a fantasy standard to fairy tales.[12] Of importance here is that the young girl, for various reasons, perceives her mother as antagonist and wishes her out of the way. An actual confrontation between mother and daughter occurs a few nights later. Again, the impulse behind this confrontation is sexual: the young girl asserts her claim to territory held by older women. Awakened by noises from her insomnia-prone mother, Allison decides to model the silk dress that she is to wear on her first date. She looks at herself in the mirror, and, upset with her childish appearance, runs to her bureau "and [takes] her rubber-padded brassiere from a drawer . . . for if the brassiere failed to make her look grown up, there was nothing left to try" (p. 152). Sporting store-bought breasts, Allison returns to her self-scrutiny, wondering what impression she will make on Rodney Harrington, her date. "Her mirror assured her that it would be a favorable one. The top of her new dress swelled magnificently, the fabric straining tautly against her rubber breasts, so that her waist seemed smaller and her hips more curved" (p. 153): a quick trip to the rubber-products section of the local five-and-ten provides the thirteen-year-old girl with centerfold proportions. Of course, life is not so simple; Constance interrupts Allison's self-contemplation and issues a series of commands: take off the dress, get to bed, "and give me that stupid rubber bra. . . . You look like an inflated balloon with that thing on" (p. 153). Suddenly a child once more, Allison bursts into tears. Constance refuses to relent: " 'Give,' she ordered, holding out her hand for Allison's brassiere" (p. 154). This midnight meeting between mother and daughter might serve as paradigm for intergenerational female struggle; confiscating the brassiere, Constance appropriates the sign of Allison's adult sexuality and catapults her daughter back into the tearful realm of childhood.

If, at the onset of adolescence, Allison experiences difficulties with her mother, "life with father" is no less problematic. Allison's biological father, the man after whom she is named, dies when she is three. Since she has no concrete memory of him, she may only develop a relationship with a fantasy father figure. Given the usual orientation of Allison's imagination, it is not surprising that she equates father with Prince, Prince who has gone but will return. On that evening when Constance finds Allison reading "Sleeping Beauty," Allison conflates herself with Beauty—and her father with Prince. After putting down her book, Allison spends some minutes in front of a photograph of her father: "He was handsome, wasn't he? . . . He looks just like a prince" (p. 31). Receiving little reply from her mother, Allison pursues her thoughts as she prepares for bed. When she says the "strange word" "father" to herself, the word means nothing. Only when she thinks of the photographic representation of this man, and connects it to the words "my prince," does the "image in her mind seem to take on life, to breathe, and to smile kindly at her" (p. 32). The title "my prince" magically brings the dead to life—and, just as magically, obscures familial relations. Thus, having successfully transformed "father" into "prince," Allison may fall asleep, asleep *with* her father. While Allison may hide the regressive and incestuous aspect of this transformation from herself, it is not hidden from a reader; Allison's sleep here resembles, too closely, the drugged sleep of a princess heroine, caught in the arms of a fantasy man.

After Allison begins to express interest in Norman, a boy her own age, her father still retains top billing: she "told him [Norman] about her own father, who was as handsome as a prince and the kindest, most considerate gentleman in the world" (p. 345). Even in speculations about herself and men other than her father, Allison employs a compensatory fairy tale structure. For example, she tells Norman that after she writes a bestseller and assumes celebrity status, she will have a new affair each week: "Men will be *dying* for my favors, but I'll be very, very particular" (p. 270; my italics). In other words, having played the princess and received her crown, Allison will play the Queen— who uses her power to punish men as she has been punished.

Allison's confusion about her relationship to both parents is most readily apparent in a scene that occurs not long after the scene in which she brags to Norman about her future, lethal powers over men. Returning home late from an afternoon picnic with Norman, Allison is greeted by a frantic Constance, who, in a crazed moment of fear and anger, tells her daughter the truth of her birth; Allison MacKenzie and Constance Standish were never married; daughter Allison is a bastard. The revelation has a cataclysmic effect on Allison: "Allison did not seem to be breathing at all. The girl sat *as if dead*. . . . The three figures in the MacKenzie living room were as *still* . . . as the *stiff* figures in a tableau" (p. 330; my italics). Confronted with the unexpected fact of unlicensed parental sexuality, Allison must abandon certain illusions about self and others. Stressing Allison's deathly stillness, Metalious suggests the death of the "child" in Allison. Events following Constance's revelation further suggest that this "dead child" wishes to revenge herself *on her mother*—to kill her mother for what Allison perceives to be an act of "defection" (p. 499) (the act is two-fold: engaging in an affair, *and* casting doubt on the sanctity of the father). Thus, when Allison breaks out of her stiffness, runs up to her bedroom, and discovers the "blue-faced, grotesque body of Nellie Cross hanging from the beam in [her] closet," she screams in terror not only because Nellie has committed suicide, but also because she has wished her mother dead. Nellie, the woman who replaces Constance—cooking, cleaning, ironing in the MacKenzie home while Constance works in her dress shop—serves as a perfect stand-in. Allison realizes that her wish has come true; a "mother" (that mother who has served as focus for anger Allison cannot express openly to Constance) is dead.

Allison is taken to Matt Swain's hospital in shock; she remains "in a shadow world" for three days. During these days of "vague dreaminess," of ritual death and rebirth, Allison is propelled from the realm of childish innocence into that of adult sexuality and guilt. When she awakens, she weeps—not loudly, like a child calling attention to herself, but silently, face hidden in pillow, like an adult. Doc Swain interrupts and gently insists that she tell him what bothers her: " 'I did it!' she sobbed. 'I killed Nellie!' " (p. 340). Although Swain consoles Allison, Constance's later reflection that Allison "had never been a child again after Constance had brought her home from the hospital" (p. 380) is accurate; blaming her mother for past sexual experiences (which actually involved both mother and father), then blaming herself for an apparent realization of deathly fantasies about her mother, Allison can never really return to the home she has known as a child, but must take more definite steps toward a home of her own.

In *Peyton Place,* as in fairy tale (and dream), an individual life story is repeated and refracted in the lives of numerous characters; to appreciate fully Allison's theme, we must listen as other characters—such as Selena and Constance—play variations on it. Thus, for example, precisely at the moment Allison's story appears most engrossing, Metalious devotes several chapters to Constance. Neither digression nor diversion, these chapters document an individual, but infinitely repeatable, instance of a paradigmatic fairy tale plot. Constance is introduced as a woman who, like Allison, grows up in Peyton Place, within the confines of her maternal home (her father receives no mention). At age nineteen she moves to New York, gets involved with a married man, and bears an illegitimate child. By 1933, the initial time setting of *Peyton Place,* this child is a young girl and Constance is a middle-aged "widow," increasingly at odds with her daughter. Mother Constance's ambivalent feelings about Allison run parallel to Allison's ambivalent feelings about Constance; this mother fears both sexual replacement *and* sexual duplication.[13] A clear example of the former fear occurs in a carefully constructed exchange between Constance and Allison. When daughter wishes for June and her upcoming grade-school graduation, mother, who peers into a mirror, "searching the corners of her eyes for small lines" (p. 71), replies: "No, don't hurry time, Allison. . . . You'll be thirteen next month" (pp. 71-72). Daughter advances into her sexually active years and mother feels as if she is being forced into a retreat. Locating Constance in front of a mirror, scanning her face as she discusses Allison's thirteenth birthday, Metalious plays on a scene from "Snow White"; standing before her mirror, a jealous Queen demands that the mirror announce "who's the fairest of them all" and is content with the mirror's reply until the day her stepdaughter, Snow White, becomes a woman and enters the competition.

Constance also fears sexual duplication; projecting her own past onto Allison's present, Constance imagines that daughter will reenact mother's past mistakes. Thus, during Allison's birthday party, when mother realizes that "post office" is being played, she immediately assumes that Allison will get into trouble with a boy. Constance fails to distinguish between self (the woman who "got into trouble") and daughter ("shy, withdrawn little Allison"). As a "quick picture of her daughter Allison, lying in bed with a man, flashes[es] through her mind" (p. 75), Constance directs an anger at Allison that is more appropriate to herself and Allison's father (far more likely candidates for a bedroom sketch). And later, when Constance confronts Allison with this bedroom sketch, she does so not out of a protective fear for Allison, but, as Mike Rossi points out, for herself: "You are afraid that she will turn out to be like you, that she will wind up with an illegitimate child on her hands, as you did" (p. 382).

In addition to a personal history that might prompt defensive anger and confusion, Constance, at age thirty-two, experiences what might be termed a second adolescence. Having devoted several years to "waiting for Allison to grow up," Constance finds herself yet a young woman with a nearly grown daughter—and an ever-increasing sense of restlessness. Metalious hints at the source of this restlessness early on ("at times she felt a vague restlessness within herself, [but] she told herself sharply that this was *not* sex, but perhaps a touch of indigestion" [p. 29]), and is more specific as time passes: "Constance was as unstill as the river in floodtime. She did not recognize the symptoms in herself as akin to the painful restlessness of adolescence, nor did she admit that the dissatisfied yearning within her could be a sexual one" (p. 155). Similar symptoms are attributed to Allison: "she seemed to be filled with a restlessness, a vague unrest, which nothing was able to ease" (p. 69). Emotionally, sexually, mother and daughter are *too* close; the story of one reads, uncomfortably and disconcertingly, as plagiarism from the other.

Constance spends several years "waiting for Allison to grow up"—a peculiar activity, as it puts Constance in the position of waiting for absence (once Allison is grown, she will go). Conveniently, as Allison reaches adolescence and takes her first steps away from the maternal home, Constance is supplied with an alternative presence; Mike Rossi, Prince Charming disguised as a schoolteacher, arrives in town. Like something out of the Brothers Grimm by way of Hollywood, Mike Rossi descends on Peyton Place: "Mike Rossi was a massively boned man with muscles that seemed to quiver every time he moved. . . . His arms, beneath sleeves rolled above the elbow, were knotted powerfully, and the buttons of his work shirts always seemed about to pop off under the strain of trying to cover his chest" (p. 142). Smitten by the beauty of the attractive "widow" (who suffers even more frequent attacks of "indigestion" following her introduction to Prince Charming), Mike pursues Constance, and, finally, convinces her to go swimming with him late one evening. In the dark near the water, Constance sees "Michael Rossi . . . massive, naked from the waist up, and *evil looking*" (p. 209; my italics). The scene which follows might be taken directly from "Beauty and the Beast," as Constance flees from this obviously sexual male and he presses himself upon her. This beast of nearly unbridled passion first unties the top strap of Beauty's bathing suit: "with one motion of his hand, she was naked to the waist" (p. 210). He then kisses her "brutally, torturously" and escorts her home where he can complete the rape he has begun. Constance protests. Mike slaps her across the mouth and insists upon her silence. Metalious comments: "It was like a nightmare from which she could not wake" (p. 211). But Beauty DOES wake; and when she does, it is to the realization that her stalwart refusal to give in to her rapist allows for the transformation of Beast into Prince. So, in *Peyton Place,* Mike Rossi, a man who has held himself aloof from love, now finds himself not only in love, but also, "hog tied and completely swozzled. He would wait for Constance MacKenzie if it took her fifty years to make up her mind" (p. 255). The kiss from a beastly toad, the rape, must be endured before Constance may receive her reward: to live "happily ever after." Such is one plot option for Allison: await the arrival of your prince; undergo certain sexual trials and tribulations requisite for the conversion of your prince into husband; reap the rewards of marital bliss.

But, in chapters devoted to Selena Cross, *Peyton Place* furnishes yet another variant of Beauty/Beast, the variant of nightmare. Most fairy tales contain elements of both dream and nightmare. It is not unusual to find the glamorous success of one character set off against the grisly failure of another. In "Ashputtel," for example, one sister rides off with the prince while two others, with mutilated toes and heels, return home, rejected. Or, in "The Goose Girl," princess and waiting maid, like twins, exchange positions, but by the end of the tale, the princess assumes her rightful position at the side of her royal bridegroom and the waiting maid is "thrown into a cask struck round with sharp nails and . . . two white horses [are] put to it, and . . . drag it from street to street till she is dead."[14]

If Allison's steps may duplicate those of her mother, they also may duplicate those of Selena, Allison's best friend and adopted "sister."[15] Selena, a girl from "the shacks," lives the underside of fairy tale plots— she is the sister who does not win the Prince, whose foot does not fit the shoe. Two early instances of "doubling, but with a difference," demonstrate the distinctive orientation of each girl. The first takes place in Constance MacKenzie's dress shop. When Constance allows Selena to try on a much coveted white dress, Allison's response to her friend's appearance is: "Oh, Selena. . . . You look perfectly beautiful. You look just like a fairy princess" (p. 61). Constance's perception, surely much closer to Selena's self-perception, differs from that of Allison: "She looked like a woman, thought Constance. At thirteen, she has the look of a beautifully sensual, expensively kept woman" (p. 61). The point here is that "princess" and "expensively kept woman" may be essentially one and the same; they differ in name only because

the former usually resides in a book of fantasy, the latter in a novel
of realism. A second example of divergence is located in Selena's hard-
headed and practical response to Allison's repeated requests for affir-
mation of the princely qualities of her father. Selena thinks with disgust
about the way in which Allison "moons" over a photograph and is
disturbed by Allison's insistence that she acknowledge how handsome
the missing father is: " 'He's dead—and you're better off, kid,' Selena
had wanted to say" (p. 61).

But Selena does not say the words—instead, the script demands
that Selena live out these words, that she provide Allison with an
example of the validity of her observation about the painful nature of
father/daughter relationships. Although the event that follows occurs
to Selena, we see it through Allison's eyes; the experience of one girl
is, to a considerable extent, incorporated by the other. On a Saturday
afternoon, not long after the clothing store incident, the two girls
arrange to spend their free time together, as usual. When Allison walks
to the shack inhabited by the Cross family and does not find Selena
at the appointed meeting place outside, she stands on a wooden crate
and looks through a window into the kitchen. Captivated by the scene
inside,[16] just as she might be captivated by a scene inside covers of a
book, Allison watches Lucas approach Selena, slap her, and rip off her
blouse. Then: "Allison fell off the packing crate and lay on the cold
ground. Her whole body was wet with perspiration and the world
seemed to undulate over her and around her. She panted with the
effort to fight off the blackness that threatened her from every side,
but she had to give way to the nausea that fought its way out of her
throat" (p. 85). With that, the chapter ends. Although we initially
might feel cheated out of the ending of Selena's story, such feelings
are unjustified; in giving us Allison's response, Metalious gives us that
of Selena. In other words, when Allison falls, pants, and attempts to
fight off "the blackness that threatened her from every side" Selena
does the same: the two girls, participant and participating spectator,
merge. While Selena suffers paternal penetration, Allison watches this
primal scene—and the two girls respond identically.[17] Despite "doubling" of Allison and Selena, a crucial difference remains; Selena, the
"unfavored" sister of fairy tale, must actually "sleep with the father"
and, unlike that sleep earlier imagined by favored sister Allison, Selena's sleep involves a violation so terrible that it can be described
only in terms of its effect—such is the horror of actual incest.[18]

Of course, as violence perpetrated by Beast on Beauty, the rape of Selena by Lucas parallels that of Constance by Mike. Superficially, differences exist between the two couples: as potential husband, Mike Rossi provides Constance with the raw material for a Prince Charming while Lucas Cross, already a husband, can make no such provision for Selena; while Constance and Mike prepare to "live happily ever after," Selena contemplates a life of misery. Similarities between the two couples, however, are just as striking, just as essential; dark males perpetrate rape after slapping, stripping, and silencing fair females. To ensure that this doubling does not go unnoticed, verbal repetition comes into play: both Mike and Lucas are "evil," "dark," "big"; both Constance and Selena are "naked to the waist," caught in a "nightmare." Further, when Selena pleads with Doc Swain to terminate the pregnancy that results from repeated instances of rape and he insists on knowing who "did this thing" to her, her reply functions as an implied indictment of all fathers: " 'It's my father,' said Selena Cross. She raised her head and looked Matthew Swain straight in the eyes. 'My stepfather,' she said" (p. 201). Father, stepfather, men in general: whether the knight's visor hides Lucas Cross or Mike Rossi (the frog or the "true prince") matters not at all—both are rapists, both are guilty.[19]

If, in discussing parallels between Constance and Selena, we seem to have digressed from Allison's story, it is here, in a consideration of dynamics between father and daughter, that we return to Allison and forge connections, suggested earlier, between Allison and Selena. Armed with the knowledge of her birth, Allison determines to leave Peyton Place for the city of her father: New York (it is important to note that New York, original home of Allison MacKenzie, was the city chosen by young Constance Standish, many years ago, when she left Peyton Place; daughter follows mother's footsteps presuming that she sets off on her own course). Once in New York, Allison selects a lover, Bradley Holmes, who quite clearly duplicates the man with whom Constance Standish engaged in an affair; thus, for Allison, he functions as both father figure and lover. Over and over again, Metalious insists upon Brad's age and paternal attitude. He is "forty years old, dark haired and powerfully built" (p. 489); that is, cut from the same pattern as Allison MacKenzie, Mike Rossi, *and* Lucas Cross. He first admonishes Allison. "Don't start thinking of me as your father" (p. 492) and then reassures her, "You must have known that no harm could come to you in the company of a man old enough to be your father" (p. 500). This is the man Allison pursues, the man Allison accompanies on a weekend in the country. It is only after this weekend that little girl Allison emerges from childhood into womanhood. Her emergence is not, however, predicated on the loss of her virginity—but rather, on the loss of her illusion of self as potential princess.[20] Allison's dream weekend begins romantically enough; when Brad receives her kiss, comments that she kisses like a child, and then teaches her to kiss "like a woman" (" 'Open your mouth a little,' he said, and kissed her again" [p. 501]), he appears to fit the role of white knight. His armor shines all the more brightly as he escorts virginal Allison to bed, lectures her on beauties of the flesh, and makes love to her, not once, but twice (he explains, "It is never as good as it should be for a woman, the first time. . . . This one will be for you" [p. 503]).

But on the drive home after a "weekend in bed," Allison receives a shock of an intensity equal to that she experienced upon learning of her illegitimate birth and Nellie's "wished for" death. Spinning out fantasies of a future life with Brad, she comments, " 'It would be terrible if I got pregnant,' . . . thinking that it would not be terrible at all, 'because then we'd have to get married and I'd never get any work done. We'd be spending all our time in bed' " (p. 504). Allison reproduces, thread for thread, the fantasy-web spun by her mother Constance years before: to go to New York, meet, work for, and finally marry a man of wealth and position (p. 26). But there was a rent in Constance's web; so too in that of Allison. When Brad hears Allison's outline for the future, he withdraws his hand from hers and says, "But my dear child . . . I was extremely conscientious about taking precautions against anything as disastrous as pregnancy. I am already married. I thought you knew" (p. 504). Not only already married, but with two children; Bradley Holmes (lover of Allison, father of two children), Allison MacKenzie (lover of Constance, father of Allison and of two children in Scarsdale), and Lucas Cross (lover of Selena, her stepfather, and father of two children) easily might fit into the same suit of armor. Allison responds to this news with a deathlike numbness; her body seems to be "insulated with ice." Her response strongly resembles that provoked by the earlier revelation of illicit union between Constance and papa prince: in both cases, Allison acknowledges the death of an illusion/a father with the appropriately shocked silence of a bereaved daughter. If Allison is ever to step out of the repetitive realm of fairy tale and into that of her own potentially unique reality, *both* father/prince figures must be killed off. Up to this point, Allison mistakenly assumes that in plagiarizing her life from fairy tale scripts written long ago, she may reap the rewards promised to the script's heroine; only after "the rewards" prove false does she realize that she may change plots, expel characters, and write her own story.

It is at this time that the lives of Selena and Allison flow together once more. As a benumbed Allison wanders the streets of New York on the Monday following her weekend with Brad, her eyes catch the bold letters of a headline: "PATRICIDE IN PEYTON PLACE." The patricide which makes headlines is that of Lucas by Selena, a literal patricide. But as Allison knows, another patricide has occurred in *Peyton Place;* she murders the phantom fathers of her imagination, and she feels the guilt attendant upon relinquishing an illusion.[21] After reading the headline, Allison senses that she must go home, to the trial. Athough she tells the local stationmaster that she returns because she assumes the Cross patricide "might make a good story," it is, more truthfully, Allison's interest in the chapters of her own story that motivates a return. Yet, as she knows, and as *we* know, a reading of Selena's history serves as comment upon and analogue to that of Allison; both girls hope to avoid repeating patterns set by mothers; both engage in incestuous involvements with fathers (one, literally, and under protest; the other, imaginatively, and with pleasure). Following her trial, Selena chooses to remain in Peyton Place, and although Allison censures the choice as "foolish," she does the same; without questioning her motives, Allison spends a slow summer in her home town, "sitting alone in her room and . . . walking the streets" (p. 485).[22] During this time, Allison comes to understand what she has formerly perceived as her mother's defection; with a shock, daughter realizes that what happened to mother "could happen to anyone" (p. 499—to any *woman*)—and has happened to her. Thus, one evening, Allison removes "the silver framed photograph of Allison MacKenzie which had stood for so many years on the living room mantlepiece" (p. 510), signaling to her mother that she wants to make peace. Erasing the sign of the father also indicates Allison's desire to make peace with herself: past, present, and future. It is this effort which truly occupies her over the summer. Allison must devote time to determining a new life-plot: how is she to structure her newfound freedom? Past scripts and stories most often involved the arrival of a fatherly

Prince Charming: however, having received instruction from Brad, as well as from Selena and Lucas, Allison must consider revision. It would seem that stories similar to the ones she has told Nellie Cross ("Once upon a time . . . in a land far across the sea, there lived a beautiful princess" [p. 132])[23] are no longer possible. Nor, perhaps, are stories similar to that which Allison has published in *McCall's*: "It's all about a girl who works in an advertising agency in New York. . . . This boss of hers is young and handsome and the girl can't help herself. She falls in love with him. In the end she marries him, after deciding that she loves him more than her career" (p. 377). Allison must choose; Metalious must choose. Is Allison's life, Metalious's novel, to move forward into uncharted territory, or to fall back into the already well-mapped realm of fairy tale? Here, finally, we locate the focus of all tensions within the novel; this is *the* question of *Peyton Place*. Difficulties attendant upon answering such a question are apparent not only in the lethargic weariness that weighs heavily upon Allison (p. 485) but also in the rather chaotically disturbed chronology of Metalious's last few chapters. Both Allison and Metalious feel the allure of fairy tale, but both see through its false promises, recognizing its insidious insistence on "reassuring repetition" and its problematic positioning of the "passive female."[24] This tension remains, finally, unresolved, as the final paragraphs of the novel allow for two possible readings. The more pessimistic suggests that Metalious and Allison finally opt for the security of Prince, castle, and "happily ever after." Metalious does provide Allison with her very own Prince, the perfect suitor: David Noyes, a young man who knows Allison's secrets, loves her nonetheless, and comes "all the way from New York" (p. 512) to see her.[25] When Constance tells an unsuspecting Allison that this young man awaits her at home, Allison hurries, "and when she reached Beach Street she ran all the way up the block to her house" (p. 512). "To her *house*": thus the novel ends, with heroine safely ensconced within walls of the maternal home, novelist safely ensconced within the traditional form of fairy tale, and reader—reader reassured that such are the appropriate choices of abode for women. However . . . given Metalious's insistence on a deconstruction of fairy tale, another reading of the final paragraphs is possible.[26] Unlike the traditional princess, Allison is *out* of the house when her hero arrives; active herself, she need not depend upon his kiss for an awakening. Also, Allison's activity is one of reconciliation with her birthplace prior to a leavetaking. On her way toward town,

she imagines the trees singing "Good-by, Allison! Good-by Allison!"—
and she is ready to wish them a good-by in return. Finally, running
to David, she runs *not* to a paternal prince, but to a man who, like
herself, stands at the very beginning of a writing career—a career of
active production rather than passive consumption. Thus, we might
imagine these two, not in Peyton Place, but in New York, not "happily
ever after," but struggling, struggling to banish fantasies imposed by
the past so as to construct realities for the future.[27]

Notes

1. Grace Metalious, *Peyton Place* (New York: Dell, 1956), p. 185. All further
page citations from *Peyton Place* are from this edition and will be included
within parentheses in my text.
2. Figures compiled by Alice Payne Hackett and James Henry Burke in
Eighty Years of Bestsellers (New York: R. R. Bowker Co., 1977) place Metalious's novel tenth on a combined (hardcover and paperback) listing of all
bestsellers in America between 1895 and 1975. Over 10,600,000 copies have
been sold (p. 10).
3. The ambition of a twentieth-century housewife, "to write and be a celebrity," differs considerably from that of the nineteenth-century "mad scribbling woman." The latter, almost without exception, wrote to alleviate pressing
financial needs; if she did not turn out so many pages a week, her family did
not eat. As Nina Baym, in *Woman's Fiction: A Guide to Novels by and about
Women in America 1820–1870* (Ithaca: Cornell University Press, 1978), notes:
the nineteenth-century woman saw "authorship as a profession rather than
a calling, as work and not art" (p. 32).
4. For a critical, rather than novelistic, analysis of fairy tales' pernicious
presentation of woman's estate, see Karen E. Rowe's "Feminism and Fairy
Tales," in *Women's Studies* 6 (1969), pp. 237-57. Two sentences from Rowe's
final paragraph must serve as brief summary here: "Whether expressed in
pornographic, domestic, and gothic fictions or enacted in the daily relations
of men and women, fairy tale visions of romance . . . continue to perpetuate
cultural ideals which subordinate women. As a major form of communal or
'folk' lore, they preserve rather than challenge the patriarchy" (p. 253).
5. See Tania Modleski's "The Disappearing Act: A Study of Harlequin Romances," *Signs* 5 (1980), p. 435, for a description of the effect of those
Harlequin romance commercials that show "a middle-aged woman lying on
her bed holding a Harlequin novel and preparing to begin what she calls her
'disappearing act.' "
6. Rowe, p. 239.

7. For example, Phyllis Hogan, writing in the *San Francisco Chronicle,* on September 28, 1956, complains that Metalious "has written far too many words, most of them undistinguished, about too many people. She has humor, heart, vigor, a feeling for irony (as well as unblushing candor and a relentless flow of profanity), all of which might have made a better showing in a simpler vehicle—say, merely, 'The Story of Selena Cross' " (p. 17). Obviously, Hogan would dispute my position that all these words, all these stories, are essential to the novel as they build off one another.

8. Interestingly enough, the plots for various characters (Allison, Selena, Constance) follow—precisely—the syntax outlined by V. Propp as characteristic of the fairy tale as a form: a family member absents himself from home (father MacKenzie); an interdiction is addressed to the heroine (no sleeping with father); the interdiction is violated (Sleeping Beauty fantasies); a villain attempts to deceive heroine/victim (mother Constance) and so forth. See V. Propp, *Morphology of the Folktale* (Austin: University of Texas, 1977), pp. 25-65.

9. When the sanctity of Allison's private space is profaned, when Allison tells Selena, "This is a special secret place. No one ever comes here but me" (p. 58) and Selena retorts "what do you mean, no one comes here but you? Boys have been bringing girls up here ever since I can remember, at night, in cars" (p. 58), so too, by analogy, the sanctity of reading space. Behind apparently incorporeal and nearly asexual figures of romance lurk men and women of flesh and blood (perhaps in cars, at night); escape into a privatized fictional world is rendered suspect as Metalious suggests that such a world exists only in the imagination of a naive twelve-year-old girl.

10. Little Thumbling grows into a giant; Jack plants a beanstalk that assumes prodigious proportions; the goose girl travels "a great way off." For other examples of physical and situational changes attendant upon puberty, see *Grimm's Fairy Tales,* ed. Kay Webb (Harmondsworth, England: Penguin, 1974).

11. Kay Stone, "Things Walt Disney Never Told Us," *Journal of American Folklore* 88 (1975), p. 47.

12. Rowe notes that many tales portray a young girl in "the throes of oedipal ambiguities [who] seizes upon her father's indulgent affection, because it guarantees respite from maternal persecutions" (p. 243).

13. Rowe explains more generally: fairy tales "in part recreate the fears of a menopausal mother. For the aging stepmother [mother], the young girl's maturation signals her own waning sexual attractiveness and control. In retaliation they jealously torment the more beautiful virginal adolescent who captures the father's affections and threatens the declining queens" (p. 241).

14. For the "Ashputtel" story, see *Grimm's Fairy Tales,* pp. 153-60; for "The Goose Girl," see *Grimm's Fairy Tales* pp. 133-40.

15. As Nellie serves as stand-in for Allison's mother, Nellie's daughter functions as Allison's step-sister.

16. Metalious describes Allison's fascination in detail: "She knew that she should get down from the packing crate and stop eavesdropping, but she was held still by something in Lucas's face, a sly and evil something that held her motionless, just as a horror movie holds a frightened child to his theater seat in spite of his fear" (p. 82). The comparison of Allison's fixation to that of a child, who cannot remove his/her eyes from a theater screen, is perfect. It reminds us of Allison's marginal age status (is she child or adult, girl or woman?); it suggests Allison's own proclivity for converting life to stories of life (which is precisely what similes and screens, distancing devices, accomplish); and it adds to a sense of fear originally stimulated by the notation of something sly and evil in Lucas's face.

17. Lucas corroborates my hypothesized account of Selena's response when he describes the rape to Doc Swain (pp. 224-25).

18. Interestingly, Allison attempts to distance herself from the *essential* horror of this scene by conflating it with the scene from a book:

soon afterward she saw a book with a paper jacket showing a slave girl with her wrists bound over her head, naked from the waist up, while a brutal-looking man beat her with a cruel-looking whip. That, she concluded, was what had been in Lucas Cross's mind on the afternoon that she had stared through his kitchen window. (P. 132)

The book jacket allows for a protective displacement of father/daughter to master/slave, of the act of rape to that of beating.

19. Selena's reply also functions as a critique of the fairy tale reward system: what sort of prize are women being offered? and for undergoing what sort of ordeal?

20. By "princess" I intend the female child who, through no act of her own but merely through her *being* (i.e., being born, being beautiful), merits the attentions of the male world—most specifically, of the male prince who has the power to elevate her from the masses to the unique position she "deserves": venerated Queen. Marcia R. Lieberman, in " 'Some Day My Prince Will Come': Female Acculturation through the Fairy Tale," *College English* 34 (Dec. 1972), clarifies this point: "Since the heroines are chosen for their beauty (*en soi*), not for anything they do (*pour soi*), they seem to exist passively until they are seen by the hero, or described to him. They wait, are chosen, and are rewarded" (p. 386).

21. Metalious uses subtle situational reverberations to draw the two young women together. After Selena murders Lucas, she tastes blood on her lips:

She licked her lips and tasted blood. "I cut my lip," she said stupidly.

Joey shook his head. "It's from him," he whispered. "It's all over you. You're covered with blood." (P. 411)

Allison tastes the same, after she is sexually penetrated by Brad: "In the last moment a bright drop of blood appeared on her mouth, where she had bitten into her lip, and then she had cried out the odd, mingled cry of pain and pleasure."

22. Allison's period of sitting and walking parallels an earlier period of life when she also roams "the streets of the town with an air of searching" (p. 71). As Metalious describes this search, it is apparent that Allison's object is the lost father: only after praying "that her father might be returned to her" and receiving no reply, does Allison start her rambles, rambles that leave "her with a hollow feeling of loss when she pulled herself up short and asked herself what she was looking for" (p. 71). An older Allison searches, more appropriately, for the self she feels she has lost.

23. The split between MacKenzies and Crosses might be exemplified in stories told (or alluded to) by members of each family. While Allison spins tales of "once upon a time," Nellie talks about Lucas, "booze and women." As she comments: "I could tell you some stories, honey, that ain't nothin' like the stories you tell me" (p. 185).

24. Rowe again provides helpful commentary: " 'Romance' glosses over the heroine's impotence: she is unable to act independently or self-assertively; she relies on external agents for rescue; she binds herself first to the father and then the prince; she restricts her ambitions to hearth and nursery" (p. 239).

25. It is no accident that David, a figure who functions for Allison as Mike Rossi functions for Constance, arrives from afar and seeks Allison in her *maternal* home: as Noyes repeats Rossi, Allison repeats Constance.

26. It should also be noted that only a few pages before this final scene, Metalious issues yet another warning about the dangers of fairy tale forms for women. In presenting Clayton Frazer's account of Samuel Peyton's castle (a castle at the heart of the novel, of gothic and of fairy tale structures) Metalious-Cassandra presents a parable directed to her women readers. Frazer relates a story of the black man, Samuel Peyton, who escapes from slavery, marries a white woman ("frail lookin' like a piece of china" [p. 455]) and then entombs her within the castle he builds: "Vi'let went first. Some say she had the consumption, and there's others say she just faded away from bein' cooped up in the castle" (p. 457): dark men, fair women, castle walls—lovely, but for women, lethal.

27. This reading, I believe, is perfectly in keeping with the text of Metalious's first novel. It is not keeping with her second, *Return to Peyton Place* (New York: Dell, 1959), where Metalious panders to her public and replays—literally—the fantasies of *Peyton Place*.

— 4 —

Valley of the Dolls: "Wow! What an Orgy!"

> Damn, damn. . . . Damn Anne's mother! Damn all mothers! Even in
> death they reached out and loused you up.
> > —Jacqueline Susann, *Valley of the Dolls*

> Matrophobia can be seen as a womanly splitting of the self, in the
> desire to become purged once and for all of our mothers' bondage,
> to become individuated and free. The mother stands for the victim
> in ourselves, the martyr. Our personalities seem dangerously to blur
> and overlap with our mothers'; and, in a desperate attempt to know
> where mother ends and daughter begins, we perform radical surgery.
> > —Adrienne Rich, *Of Woman Born*

One of the most appealing aspects of *Peyton Place* is Metalious's
depiction of her heroine's struggle to come to terms with herself and
her surroundings. Unappreciated by the general populace of Peyton
Place, the gifted Allison MacKenzie troops off to New York City, writes
a bestseller, and shows them all—just like the author of her story,
whose best-selling novel proved a lesson to the populace of her own
native town, Manchester, New Hampshire. Ten years later, in another
woman's bestseller destined to break records and shock the reading
public, we encounter a heroine, Anne Welles, whose initial situation
runs a close parallel to that of Allison MacKenzie. Like Allison, Anne
grows up in an exclusively female home in a small New England town.
Feeling unappreciated and at odds with her mother and with the towns-
folk, Anne, like Allison, escapes: first, imaginatively, into works of
literature and then, actually, to "the big city," New York.[1] Here, how-

ever, paths pursued by Allison and Anne diverge; the former, a heroine from the nineteen-fifties, writes her own book; the latter, a heroine from the sixties, types a book written by her lover. Although this distinction may be stated too baldly, it is, essentially, true: the former struggles to produce her own work; the latter submits to reproduction of the work of others.

Certainly, given popular conceptions of women's socioeconomic roles during these two decades, the career choices made by the two heroines come as a surprise. One would expect more authority from the heroine of the sixties, who exists in a decade when the number of women entering the work force tops the number of those remaining home, when President John Kennedy appoints a commission on "the status of women, whose espoused purpose was to determine how the American economy could better utilize the talents of women," and when Betty Friedan publishes *The Feminine Mystique* (which "blasted the icon of '50s domesticity"), then aids in the birth of the National Organization of Women.[2] Perhaps it is precisely in its ambivalent reaction to these issues of the sixties that *Valley of the Dolls* so strongly appeals to women who are similarly ambivalent. *Valley does* show signs of its time; as Susann tells the tale of Anne Welles and her two other heroines, Neely O'Hara and Jennifer North, she documents, in detail, the interaction of American women and a post-war (1945-65), consumption-oriented economic system.

Interestingly, this documentation might serve as fictional exemplum of conditions described by American feminists as most oppressive to women—but as Susann compiles case studies of unhappy women, she takes care to avoid suggesting (as almost any feminist would suggest) that the origins of female woe lie in an oppressive patriarchal culture. No, the monster lurking in Susann's *Valley*—an apparently "natural monster," transcending time and place, bearing an uncanny resemblance to the monsters in folktale, fairy tale, and gothic romance—is female, and she responds to the name "mother." Combining a radical presentation of America's sexual economic system (in which women consume or are consumed, but never produce) and a reactionary explanation of this system (mothers fail to nourish daughters properly), *Valley* assures its female audience that emotional and sexual malnutrition are the norm for women, that relief comes not through systemic change but through some unimaginable change in mother-daughter relations, and finally, that as the latter *is* unimaginable, the norm must be maintained. In other words, if you are a woman-born-of-woman, it is normal that you feel underfed, just as it is normal that you engage in voracious consumption (another novel by Susann, perhaps?) as compensation. Thus, while Susann, like Metalious, may delight in authorial defiance (Susann's novel raised the same, if somewhat grayer, eyebrows as Metalious's) the novelist of the sixties, unlike her predecessor, does not encourage defiance on the part of her heroines or her readers.

When Tom Nairn, in *New Statesman,* attributes *Valley's* popularity to the fact that it is "a sick woman's book, through and through"[3] he is right on target; but when he chides *Valley* for saying "nothing about society or history" during the twenty-year span of its narrative, his critical arrow falls short. Susann's novel may say little about society and history in "The Great Tradition," but it speaks at length about society and history as lived by American women from 1945 to 1965. In the pages that follow, I am interested first, in analyzing those aspects of society and history, depicted in *Valley,* that necessitate female sickness, and second, in suggesting ways in which Susann eventually conspires with the doctors in control, calmly pats her reader-patients on the head, and writes a prescription, ever-renewable, for placebos.

The lingerie ad 'Be Some Body' isn't just a cute play on words. It is precisely the advertising message: a woman is supposed to be a body, not a person—a decorated body. If she can successfully manage that transformation, then she can market herself—for a man.[4]

As a former actress, playwright, and television star, Susann knows the importance of an opening scene, a scene that focuses an audience's attention, suggests themes, and sets the tone for what follows. *Valley of the Dolls* opens in an employment agency specializing in jobs for "girls." The setting allows for the introduction of issues that will be pursued throughout the novel: what do women have to sell? who buys what they sell? what compensation do they receive? Only one of Susann's three major heroines checks in with the agency, but, given that all three share a situation of under- or unemployment at the novel's beginning, Anne's experience may be taken as typical.

It is September, 1945, when Anne Welles arrives in New York, the city of her dreams. She immediately applies to an agency for work. The inexperienced but obviously attractive Anne is told by a "girl" at the agency that even without experience, she will have no trouble getting a job. The girl then advises Anne that with looks like hers, "I'd head straight for John Powers or Conover."[5] Learning that Powers and Conover are modeling agencies, however, Anne declines and insists that she would like to work in an office. The female agent then hands Anne several slips of paper, advising her that Henry Bellamy might be her best lead, as he is a big theatrical attorney and his secretary just married John Walsh. Reacting to Anne's lack of reaction, the agent informs her about the impressive John Walsh and then adds that since Anne's looks far exceed those of Myrna, who married John, Anne is bound to "grab a live one right away" (p. 2). Confused once again, Anne must ask about what sort of "live one" the agent has in mind, and the agent responds, "Guy . . . maybe even a husband" (p. 2). This exchange of questions and answers reads almost like a dialog between natives of two different countries; repeatedly, Anne betrays ignorance of key words and common assumptions. In responding to Anne, the employment agent instructs her and us in elementary post-war sexual economics: a girl works temporarily, until procuring a man, then leaves the work force to be replaced by yet another unattached girl. Further, in this market, unlike that during the war, girls do better selling their "looks" rather than their labor. The casual use of this colloquial plural noun (of somewhat dubious parentage: do women have looks independent of men, or because men look at them?) somewhat belies its importance—importance as it delineates the product women are to sell: looks, a look, an image.

On the basis of her looks, Anne gets the job: "Henry Bellamy couldn't believe his *eyes*" (p. 6; my italics). Later, when it comes time to move on to something slightly different, she gets another job—on the basis of the same qualifications. And even later, when Anne exchanges an employer for a husband, the latter selects Anne, again, on similar grounds. This husband explains that his other romances failed, because the women with whom he was involved could not live up to Anne's "image" (p. 425). Obviously, advice given Anne by our female employment agent holds true: market your looks. Anne's husband, Lyon Burke, merely refines this advice, specifying a particular look, an image. But what particular look sells? And what is the effect of catering your product to the demand of a male audience? Throughout the careers of Anne Welles, Jennifer North, and Neely O'Hara, these questions are asked and answered, over and over again.

Certainly, beauty is one ingredient of "the look," but a more basic, particularly American ingredient, is youth. The director of Jennifer's films attributes her appeal to an American freshness and youthfulness. Youth forms the basis of Neely's attractiveness as well; audiences crave "the bright-eyed girl," "the fresh-faced child." Specifying "looks" as women's most marketable commodity, specifying youth as the basic index of this commodity, the system portrayed in *Valley* tragically limits a female's period of possible success. Reviewer Tom Nairn may castigate *Valley* as a "timeless, self-regarding universe, [in which] the America of 1945-65 disappears effortlessly: time signifies only ageing, and a growing, incurable anxiety about wrinkles and fat."[6] Yet he might better castigate the America of 1945-65, in which the movement of time, for 51 percent of the population, *can* signify nothing other than ageing and a growing anxiety about wrinkles and fat. Without end, male characters remind females that only a young face can be attractive. Allen Cooper is most explicit: "This is a man's world—women only own it when they're very young" (p. 161). Lyon Burke expresses similar sentiments. When he tells Anne that if you lose one girl you may replace her with another, he prefaces this statement with an observation about the nature of time: "time is life. It's the only thing you can never get back" (p. 38). As usual, Lyon speaks in clichés, but his trite pronouncement applies to women in an especially lethal fashion: certainly, time is life, but, even more certainly, time is death. Given that the essence of the feminine image is youth, any woman who is no longer a girl is also, presumably, no longer a woman. (Interestingly, this privileging of girlhood effectively denies motherhood as a productive option; as we will see later, this is only one of many matrophobic impulses recorded in the novel.) Anne also receives a tutorial session on this subject from George Bellows. When Anne innocently mentions to George that as a young girl she loved the actress Helen Lawson, George cautions her to avoid all references to age when in Helen's presence. He instructs Anne that in the law office they treat Helen as if she were twenty-eight. Completely taken aback Anne protests that surely Helen is too intelligent to think she looks like a little girl. George simply shrugs his shoulders and volunteers to call Anne in twenty years and ask her how *she* feels. Poor Helen must take her place with all those silly ladies who go to ridiculous lengths to deny their years. But also, poor Anne: George hints that even she may come to share Helen's fate. Although George does not phone Anne twenty years later, Susann allows us to; twenty years after this exchange the novel ends with Anne's not-so-rosy assessment of what it means to be a forty-year-old woman.

But we see the effects of time on Helen long before we hear about them from Anne. In some ways, the ageing singer, introduced early in the novel, provides a paradigm for Anne, Jennifer, and Neely; she plots a sequence of chapters for them. Once a "hot commodity," much in demand, Helen now shows signs of age; watching her perform, Anne notices a thickness around Helen's waist, a spreading at her hips, and feels she is looking upon "the cruel distortion of a monument" (p. 82). Girdles of iron cannot squeeze Helen back into the monumental mold that goes by the name "American girl" and definitive notice of Helen's failure in the image market arrives with the news that she must pay the way for her dates, rather than the reverse. Following Helen's footsteps most closely, too closely, is Susann's heroine Neely O'Hara, who appears initially as a fresh-faced kid, but whose age, at the novel's end, must roughly correspond to Helen's age at the novel's outset. Like Helen, Neely has talent, but she markets this talent in a package designed to further encourage sales: here's the singer of youth. Also like Helen, Neely learns that as years go by the package becomes a prison: who wants an old female singer? And, after repeated suicide attempts, Neely lands in a very real prison: Haven Manor, a psychiatric center. Even here, female youthfulness assumes privileged status, as one doctor explains that his goal in therapy is to return "a *bright-eyed, talented girl* to the world" (p. 388; my italics. This is said about a thirty-three-year-old woman.)[7] Anne and Lyon express their desired perception of Neely in similar terms: Anne insists that the "real Neely" is "the *bright-eyed child*" (p. 343; my italics) with whom she shared an apartment-house on Fifty-Second Street, and Lyon, assigned to do an article on the singer, refuses to visit her, preferring to "remember her as she was, as the *fresh-faced child*" (p. 445; my italics).

Susann's use of the verb "remember" is interesting here, as it suggests that Lyon, like Neely's psychiatrist, must put "the pieces" (members) back together again. Further, it calls to mind a statement made by Kevin Gilmore, only a few pages earlier, also about women and time. Threatened by the return of Lyon, Anne's former lover, Kevin declares that Anne, as a woman in her late thirties, has passed her prime. Lyon may have loved her when she was younger, but even then, he walked out on her, leaving Kevin to "pick up the pieces" (p. 431). In other words, once past her girlish twenties, a woman degenerates, progressively, into "pieces": tired eyes, flabby thighs, multiple chins. While delivering this death blow (Anne is in her late thirties!), Kevin clearly articulates yet another effect of the systematic reduction of women's marketable resources; given intense focus on the female body as image, this body loses its wholeness and splits into pieces, each of which may be appraised independently. Throughout *Valley* we are exposed to repeated examples of a curious disjunction of female body parts. Occasionally, these examples are comic but, even in comedy, they express potential tragedy: the tragedy of a lost integrity.

We can follow the shift from comedy to tragedy in three "women's room" scenes. In each of these, Anne and another woman leave male escorts for the shelter of a powder room. In the first such scene, Anne is prompted by Helen, who encourages her toward "the little girls' room" where they "fix their faces" (p. 92). Helen's reference to the woman's room as "little girls' room" is perfectly in keeping with her desire to knock twenty years from her age, as is her use of the verb phrase "fix our faces." The verb suggests not only that the faces of these women need to be repaired, but also, that they need to be held in place, stationary against time's ravages. Granted, the language employed in this scene is cliché-ridden, but it is precisely the language of cliché that reveals most about the value system of the novel. Jennifer uses the same words, to the same effect, in a later scene with Anne. After suggesting that she and Anne go "powder their noses," Jennifer advises Anne to take a job offered her by Kevin Gilmore, then urges Anne to "fix" her face so as to avoid losing the job before she gets it. Fix your face, fix your face: clearly, if you are a woman you are susceptible to *un*-fixing, to coming apart. The third women's room scene renders this susceptibility graphically. This time, while Neely and Anne powder their noses, they meet Helen, who intends to do the same. The two singers, who, like mother and daughter, resemble each other too closely for an easy relationship, hurl insults at each other. Neely delivers a fatal blow, however, when she grabs Helen's hair and the hair—a wig—comes off in her hands. After holding up the black hair like some sort of trophy, Neely dashes into a toilet stall and attempts to flush away the wig for good. A mutilated Helen, figuratively castrated, literally "unfixed," cannot go back into the nightclub until all patrons have left; fragmented, she remains a prisoner of the little girls' room.

Neely may delight in mama Helen's imprisonment, but the delight proves short-lived, as Neely soon receives a similar sentence. Like Helen, Neely participates in a system of female commodification that eventually results in female disintegration; Neely too suffers an "unfixing," a falling into pieces. An early, casual comment from Anne provides a key for an understanding of this process as it affects Neely. Listening to the singer's first album, Anne comments, "Hey, Neely's *stuck*" (p. 214; my italics). Anne is right; as a woman entering the media market, Neely is stuck, stuck in a scale that permits the repetition of only a very few notes over and over again. Ironically, as Neely's albums, stories, photographs, and films proliferate, the woman herself is more confined; laces of the "American girl's" straitjacket are pulled all the more tightly. When, for example, Neely decides to divorce her husband, a studio boss opposes her decision on the ground that divorce would be bad for her image. Audiences want to see Neely as the girl next door—and the girl next door does *not* get a divorce. Certainly, male media personalities also find themselves trapped in particular images, but at least their selection of traps is far wider than that offered to females who, in Susann's novel, are shown only one model: American girl. As the media play on this single image/single aspect of Neely, Neely's whole self falls apart; the woman cracks. Neely's suicide attempts, however, merely catapult her into yet another particularly female prison: the expensive psychiatric center.[8] Sadly, when Neely protests that she cannot be kept in a "two-by-four-cage" at Haven Manor, she fails to see that cages outside the manor make use of far tighter security systems. Further splitting of this woman then occurs as she engages in typical psychiatric behavior: checking in and out of the hospital, gaining and losing weight, suffering addiction to and withdrawal from pills.

Neely's disintegration begins on a psychological plane; that of Jennifer, on a physical plane. In almost every description of the latter, an impersonal synecdoche reigns. When Anne, for example, sees Jennifer for the first time, she focuses on "the face": "*It* was a perfect face. . . . *The* eyes seemed warm and friendly, and *the* short, straight nose belonged to a beautiful *child*" (p. 64; my italics). This face appears to exist on its own, independent of a personality. It does not belong to a "her"; its eyes, nose, and teeth will not brook a third person possessive adjective. Further, the face floats independently of "the body"—yet another part. Anne notes that this face seems unaware of "the commotion *the body* was causing. . . . *The body* and its *accoutrements* continued to pose but *the face* ignored the furor and greeted people" (p. 64; my italics). Despite apparent praise for body and face, this language reads awkwardly, uncomfortably, and suggests a schizophrenic splitting of the whole person. Other descriptions of Jennifer continue this process of fragmentation. Jennifer's film director, for example, responds to Jennifer's assertion of self with the comment that this "self" is simply a face and a pair of breasts. Jennifer herself performs a curious split-and-double operation when she strokes her breasts and coos to Tony: "Marry *us* tonight, Tony. *We* want to belong to you" (p. 219; my italics). Like Helen, like Neely, Jennifer makes money off her "parts" and, like Helen and Neely, finds herself caught in her own skin. When Jennifer observes that her face and breasts win her contracts but deny her the possibility of belief in true love, when she submits to an eight-day "rest cure" to take inches off her waistline, when she undergoes facial surgery at Clinique Plastique to lift sagging muscles, individual body parts take precedence over the whole. Ultimately, the whole suffers; Jennifer is sentenced to the disease of proliferating parts: cancer. As images of Jennifer's breasts multiply on film, in magazines, wildly metastasizing cells within those breasts do the same. When Jennifer's doctor diagnoses her tumor as malignant and prescribes immediate removal of the breast, various effects of sexually defined commodification (duplication, fragmentation, dismemberment, imprisonment) come together and find a perfect metaphor in the disease that consumes so many American women each year. And when the doctor delivers his verdict, Jennifer hears a death sentence: only an inessential "non-self" would remain following removal of the breast.[9] So Jennifer resorts to a lethal overdose of sleeping pills, maintaining the wholeness of her various parts, at the expense of her life.

A few years later, upon giving birth to a daughter, Anne names her child after the deceased film star. This tribute serves as innocent example of yet another potentially lethal effect of a reduction of women's marketable resources: an assumption of easy replaceability. In a system where women sell only "a look," packaging assumes priority, distinctions underneath the package go unappreciated, and consumers come to believe that what is inside one attractively decorated box is as good as what is inside another. Lyon Burke expresses this sentiment to Anne in a remark quoted earlier: "You can lose a girl and perhaps win her back—or find another" (p. 38). Lyon is not the first to make reference to this easy purchase policy (no deposit/no return); *Valley* opens with the suggestion of infinite female replaceability as the employment agent urges Anne to fill in for Myrna, a woman who, undoubtedly, filled in for the woman before her. Given an economy in which humans are reduced to functions (the typist, the stenographer, the programmer) such replacements are not particularly extraordinary, and would not merit mention were it not for the fact that in *Valley*, these oft-discussed replacements affect only one sex.[10] Other early examples of an assumption of simple substitution occur as Anne spends time with men who can afford to buy girls, one after another. At El Morocco with Allen Cooper, his father Gino, and Adele (Gino's "showgirl" girlfriend), Anne observes numerous "girls who looked like exact replicas of Adele" (p. 47), replicas who may fill in for Adele when Gino tires of her. And, if Adele-replicas are to be found, surely Anne-replicas are not out of the question—or so assumes Henry Bellows, Anne's boss, upon hearing reports of her engagement to Allen. Henry prepares to call the employment agency to send over a new girl until Anne interrupts him. She expresses her indignation both at his expectation that she is going to leave and at his assumption that she is so easily replaceable. Henry then vows that no one can follow Anne, but his vow is deflated not long after, when Anne actually does resign. Accepting her resignation, Henry comments that she is one in a million, then tells her to scram because he has to call the agencies. "Who knows, maybe another Anne Welles might walk in" (p. 279). Within two sentences, Henry performs a complete turnaround: from asserting that Anne is one in a million, he hypothesizes that another Anne may walk through the door.[11] Further, if Henry may find a replacement for Anne as secretary, Allen may find a replacement for her as fiancée and eventual wife. A few years after Anne rejects the wealthy playboy's marriage proposal, she meets him with the "attractive young girl" he does marry. Anne notes the girl's large emerald-cut diamond, a diamond identical to the one Allen once had given to Anne. Studying the ring worn by her replacement, Anne muses that perhaps Allen has a drawerful of such rings, lying in wait for the proper girl and proper occasion. The point here is the novel's insistence upon the ready availability of "girls"; Allen may have a drawerful of them as well.

A young Anne may muse upon such instances of replacement; a young Neely structures her career around them. Neely's first break occurs when The Gaucheros, a three-person song and dance team of which she is a member, receives a part in a Broadway musical, "Hit the Sky." But Neely's hopes hit the floor when she discovers that Helen Lawson, star of the show, intends to perform Neely's part in the song and dance team; Helen, effectively, replaces Neely. Neely then learns that Anne has been befriended by the middle-aged star; she urges Anne to tell Helen about Anne's "second-best friend." In reply, Anne smiles and assures Neely that no one could replace her. Of course, Neely appeals to Anne precisely because she has been replaced. Further, Neely's appeal succeeds only because Anne suggests to Helen that Neely replace yet another young actress, Terry Knight, for whom Neely has been understudy. As Neely's career soars, she leaves the show and is replaced by her own understudy, Irma; the cycle begins again. While Neely can fetch a good price, she determines which women she will oust, which women she will allow. But when Neely's stock takes a fall, she is pushed out of the spotlight. Despite disclaimers from her Hollywood producer that he is not replacing Neely with Janie Lord ("No one could replace Neely O'Hara" [pp. 314-15]), Neely, like Anne, must move aside as a young substitute takes her place. The impact of such configurations of replacement is to convince us, once more, of the truth of Lyon Burke's words; one woman, like laundry detergent, easily may stand in for another.

Actually, Susann provides most damning evidence of the pervasiveness of Lyon's attitude with references to mass media's perversion of the Cinderella story—traditionally, a story that insists upon female individuality: the foot of only *one* woman will fit the shoe. Although Susann, unlike Metalious, is not intent upon a detailed manipulation of fairy tale, she does make reference to the Cinderella story in particularly disturbing ways. The first such reference occurs in connection with Anne and suggests media's tendency to generalize and commodify the fairy tale, undermining its very essence. After an evening with Gino and Allen Cooper at El Morocco, Anne awakes to the headlines: "Broadway's Newest Cinderella—Allen Cooper to Wed Secretary" (p. 52). Worthy of note in this headline is the fact that Anne is merely the "newest" Cinderella; obviously, Cinderellas come and go, are replaced by other Cinderellas. This perversion of the fairy tale allows for mass market appeal, as does the use of a generalized occupational description ("secretary") rather than specific denomination of the newest Cinderella (*not* "Allen Cooper to Wed Anne Welles"). The headline seems to promise Anne a life of "happily ever after," but such is not the case in modern-day media land. Instead, Anne is surrounded by reporters as she walks into the office. She feels trapped in a childhood nightmare as media men pounce on her, furiously asking questions and snapping photographs. To be Cinderella: the assumption of this role requires that Anne be shot at, shot down upon, encased and enclosed, commodified and splashed on front pages, identified as an image rather than as a self.[12]

Susann's second Cinderella reference, less specific but no less deflationary, occurs only a few pages later. When Henry Bellamy mentions Jennifer North and Anne does not know whom he is talking about, Henry explains that Jennifer has been top newsmaker during the last few days. Arriving "from nowhere," she is courted by and marries a prince, only to file for an annulment four days later. Such is the storyline for modern Cinderellas: leave your humble hearthstones, make media news, but, once more, do *not* live happily ever after. Ironically, Jennifer is the "old Cinderella," knocked off the front pages by the "newest Cinderella," Anne. Also ironically, Jennifer's narrative within the novel actually begins a few chapters after the traditional fairy tale ends; instead of securing her prince and settling in the castle, Jennifer discovers that the royal money is made of tin and the royal family plans to market her American charm, so she resigns her part and turns to other things. When Jen's narrative— certainly more in the tradition of gothic horror than fantasy and fairy tale—does come to a close, her name makes headlines once again as the newspapers run her life story. Unaware of this story's tragic next-to-last chapter, they print a "Cinderella" version, given to them by Jen's mother. The story that Jennifer's mother spreads is in keeping with Jen's success as a film star and image-maker; no mention is made of Jennifer's cancer, of the cancer at the heart of this commodification system.

We, as readers, however, know—know that according to economic laws governing *Valley*, a woman must sell herself as an image but, that as this image is subject to reproduction and proliferation, the woman is subject to a loss of self, a loss of integrity. As the novel moves through the 1950's and into the 1960's, the pace of this production of female images accelerates wildly; Neely reads about Jen in *Look*, cannot open a magazine without seeing Anne's picture, and plans to watch Anne do Gillian Cosmetics commercials on television.

And as Neely's producer warns her that this last form of media may spell death for individual films (he compares television to cancer, spreading everywhere), we know that it, along with other forms of mass commodification, may spell death for individual women as well. Despite the hard sell, there are no Cinderellas in this novel.

Make the rest of the afternoon count. Buy a new dress, have your hair done— or do any of the wonderful things a beautiful girl should do. (P. 39)

Up until now, discussion of women and marketing within *Valley* has focused upon women as products to be consumed—that is, women as they engage in the selling of self as representative of a particular look or image. Not surprisingly, *Valley* also implicates women, much more than men, as consumers within this system. When Kevin Gilmore notes that Gillian cosmetics employs Anne to proliferate an image of cosmetic beauty, he stresses that this image is aimed at women, women who will consume lipstick, eye shadow, and mascara so as to reproduce the face they see on the TV screen. For quite a long time, advertisers have agreed that although,women may lack real financial power, they do exert purchasing power—so ads are directed at the fickle female.[13] Susann, in *Valley*, provides more than a simple restatement of this assessment. Certainly, the three females in *Valley* indulge in a considerable amount of consumption: Jennifer buys clothes; Neely buys caviar; Anne buys a legal firm—and all three buy pills. But with these heroines Susann also approaches an understanding of the sexual dynamics of labor (dynamics that discourage women from assuming productive positions) and depicts a familial structure in which little girls, much more than little boys, are trapped in the role of never-satisfied consumer, a role that then cannot be abandoned in later life.

Early in the novel (1945), Lyon, always one to hit upon essentials, summarizes the split between spheres of female consumption and male production. He tells Anne that the night before he was out with a beautiful creature who talked to him about the hardships she had endured during the war. This woman, deprived of bobby pins and plastic lipstick containers, expresses her satisfaction over the deployment of the atomic bomb; according to Lyon, she was "down to her last six pairs [of nylons] when it hit" (p. 38). While complimenting this female creature on her beauty, Lyon expresses scorn for her extremely limited world view; wrapped up in herself, in nylons and plastic, the woman displays no awareness of the effect of the atom bomb except as it allows her to purchase, once more, the stockings that will attract men like Lyon to her. Assuredly, Lyon's scorn is merited, but his analysis really does not go far enough. He does not ask, as we must ask, if this beauty possesses the option for a response other than that of consumer.

Susann draws the line of demarcation between those who produce and those who consume most clearly when women, who belong to the latter group, plead for admission to the former. Anne, for example, wants to "labor." Once she has procured a job, however, she quickly is made aware of its parameters. Rather than engage in an act of primary production, she is confined to the consumption, then secondary reproduction of the words of others. She describes her function in Henry's office as "a human Dictophone," taking in the statements made by clients as they take in food and drink. This description also might apply to Anne's functions outside the office as she tells Lyon that she will spend weekends with him, typing up the pages of his manuscripts. Quite simply, it is men who produce, women who consume and reproduce. Susann's decision to grant Lyon authorial laurels is noteworthy, in light of earlier comments about *Peyton Place,* a novel of the fifties, in which a woman assumes authority and writes her own text. Interestingly, by 1966, Susann feels more comfortable with a much more conservative presentation of male authority and female subservience. In addition to reading Lyon's novel, Anne reads those of Hemingway, Fitzgerald, Sinclair Lewis. Further, she repeats, in her own life, one of the patterns she discerns in these authors; like them, she flees the city of her birth. But unlike these authors, Anne never *produces* an account of her flight; she merely consumes accounts produced by men.

To return, however, to the actual conditions of Anne's labor situation: after Henry's brief summary of the duties Anne will be expected to perform, we hear almost nothing about the way she spends her time in the office. Henry and Lyon may work while on the train for a New Haven opening (they open attaché cases, concentrating on legal papers and contracts), but Anne, who accompanies them, does not possess an attaché case, contracts, legal papers—or—a usual working day. While the two men produce, Anne flips through a magazine. Despite her major in English and her education at Radcliffe, Anne's magazine surely is one that contains articles about silk stockings and lipsticks and other products to be purchased by the feminine half of the population.

Anne's activity here barely qualifies as work, but at least she is on the job. Most often, when reference is made to Anne's work, it is in the form of a suggestion that she get off the job, quit permanently, or take a vacation. Repeatedly, this woman receives commands from men similar to the one from Lyon Burke quoted at the beginning of this section. Lyon insists that Anne take the afternoon off and "buy a new dress, have your hair done." When Anne protests that she wants to go back to the office, Lyon pulls rank, and *orders* her to take the afternoon off. An almost identical exchange takes place between Anne and Henry, after Henry hears rumors of a marriage between Anne and Allen Cooper. Henry assumes that Anne wants to resign and when she denies any such desire, he fires her, instructing her to marry Allen Cooper and "be happy." Allen, too, cannot understand Anne's desire to continue working. Despite reiterated statements of her intentions to keep the job and remain single, Anne must listen to Allen's expressions of doubt. He simply cannot believe that she wants to work and does not want to marry. As a listing of such exchanges might continue for pages, it is more economical to abbreviate the list and present only one final, and particularly telling example, from the mouth of Gino, Allen Cooper's father. When social columnist Ronnie Wolfe compliments Anne on her checkbones and comments that she might work as a model, Gino interrupts. He asserts that if Anne really wanted to work, he would buy her a modeling agency. "But she's gonna settle down and raise babies" (p. 44). Here, then, we come to a blatant expression of the labor ethic enunciated in *Valley:* men produce; women consume and *re*produce.

The quotation from Gino also points toward the context in which Susann locates the origins of this consumerism, a familial context of mothers and daughters. Even more basic than the reiterated suggestion that women should consume rather than produce is the reiterated presentation of daughters who *must* consume because mothers fail to supply adequate nourishment. Thus, rather than functioning as a systemic critique, *Valley,* like the many gothic novels upon which it builds, singles out the maternal figure for blame. Rather than pursuing implications suggested above (that structures of the labor system impose different roles on men and women), Susann directs her anger, and that of her readers, at an easier target: the improvident mother. In a roundabout way, the title of Susann's novel serves as signpost indicating the orientation of her critique: women in *Valley* not only are condemned to the consumption of "dolls" (pills) but also, more essentially, to a definition of self as "dolls"—as little girls who cannot grow up, caught in unsatisfying/unsatisfactory relationships with mothers and thus incapable of being good mothers themselves. Phyllis Chesler, with different ends in mind than Susann, also takes note of this phenomenon: "The way in which female children grow up—or learn how not to grow up—is initiated by the early withdrawal or relative absence of the female and/or nurturant body from their lives."[14]

While *Valley* makes virtually no reference to fathers (they are beneficently absent) and very few references to mothers and sons,[15] mothers and daughters abound; Susann suggests that her heroines Anne, Neely, and Jennifer take their cue as consumers at the breasts of their mothers. Susann draws connections between mothers' nourishment and daughters' consumption most clearly in the case of Neely, orphaned at a very young age and thus, according to the logic of the novel, craving other forms of nourishment as replacement for the maternal nourishment that she is denied. Early symptoms of Neely's tendency toward compensatory consumption occur in a scene between young Neely and Anne. As the latter leaves on a date, the former asks if Anne has any more of her terrific chocolate marshmallow cookies left. Anne offers the entire box, and Neely, "cradling the box," responds: "Oh marvelous! . . . I've got a library copy of *Gone with the Wind,* a quart of milk and all these cookies. Wow! What an orgy!" (p. 24). The message here seems obvious: never having been cradled, Neely cradles herself, surrounds herself with objects that she will consume and incorporate. The objects Neely selects—a women's bestseller, milk, and cookies—also suggest a state of emotional development arrested prior to resolution of primary needs.

Although the best-selling *Valley* certainly merits comparison to the best-selling *Peyton Place,* an even more interesting comparison may be the one suggested here by Susann—to *Gone with the Wind.* The 1936 bestseller is the only novel mentioned by name in *Valley;* further, when Neely, not long after reading Mitchell's novel, must choose a stage name for herself, she adopts Scarlett as ancestor, christening herself Neely O'Hara. Neely's choice is appropriate: both she and Scarlett live in the shadow of a large maternal figure; both experience intense pangs of hunger; both consume themselves in attempts to find nourishment. Neely's orgiastic ingestion of marshmallow cookies and Mitchell's novel serves as the first in a series of such scenes. As she grows older, her tastes become more expensive (she indulges in caviar rather than milk and cookies), but the motivation for this consumption remains the same. For example, when Neely feels abandoned by her husband, she tiptoes down to the kitchen, opens the refrigerator, removes a large jar of caviar, and assures herself that she is going to have a ball. After consuming the caviar, several pills, and a large quantity of liquor, Neely staggers to bed, leaving instructions with the butler to ward off all telephone calls. She intends "to sleep . . . and eat . . . and sleep . . . and eat . . . for maybe a week" (p. 306). "To sleep and eat": the orgy that Neely envisions for herself is the orgy of a newborn baby.[16] Despite/because of its regressive qualities, Neely's vision exerts a peculiarly strong force: to be asleep in a womblike state, to be fed upon demand: what hungry little child could ask for more?

At times, Susann specifies the source of Neely's hunger. Neely tells her director, John Sykes, that her psychiatrist has pushed her to realize that she feels the need for "mass love" because she has never known a mother's love. John scoffs and chides Neely for accepting the verdict of a fancy doctor who is bound to blame everything on the poor mothers of the world. He asks Neely if she really believes that her mother intentionally died early to punish her child. John asks a reasonable question, a question we might ask—but the novel insists that mothers *are* to blame. A few years after Neely's conversation with John, she finds herself in therapy with yet another "fancy doctor" and, sure enough, his very first question focuses on Neely's mother. He asks that Neely tell him about her mother. Neely may object that she has already spent too many years and too much money convincing her former psychiatrist that she doesn't remember her mother, but her objection merely compounds evidence against the woman who provides so little love that her daughter cannot even conjure up a memory.

If Neely's mother commits a mortal sin by dying, Jennifer's mother commits a sin of similar magnitude by living. It is Jennifer's mother who assumes the role of the mother who, having nourished her daughter, now expects nourishment in return. Interestingly, appropriately, Jen's mother looks to Jen's breasts as source of nourishment. She advises Jen to watch her weight, to keep her figure, and to make her breasts "pay" while she has them. Of course, mama intends that money earned on these mammary glands will eventually revert to her, the initial giver of milk. This intention pushes Jen even further into the role of consumer, purchasing and discarding closets of clothing so as to capture Tony Polar and thereby support the demands of her parent. Jennifer rebels, but in a rather surreptitious fashion; in a phone conversation between Jen and her mother, we learn that Jen has told Tony that her mother is dead. When Jen's very lively mother protests, Jen asks what her mother would like her to say—that Jen has a houseful of relatives just waiting to move in with her and Tony? It makes no difference whether mothers are alive or dead, nutritive or nonnutritive; in either state they damn daughters to a condition of incessant consumption. Jen learns that even in a state between life and death, mothers "louse you up." Just as she convinces Tony that he must marry her before he can enjoy her body, a telegram arrives, announcing the death of Anne's mother. This interruption ruins Jen's game with Tony (he forces himself upon her) and all Jen can do is swear silently: "Damn, damn! What timing. Damn Anne's mother! Damn all mothers! Even in death they reached out and loused you up" (p. 221). Jen's curse might serve as epigraph for Susann's novel because, in the final analysis, Susann damns mothers, damns them for both reaching and not reaching.

Jen's curse is not the last leveled at the dead Mrs. Welles. Daughter Anne curses her mother in very similar fashion following a weekend she and Lyon spend together in Lawrenceville, during which Lyon proposes that he and Anne live in the maternal house. Anne's horrified response (she feels that the house is a mausoleum, a shrine to the dead) sends a silenced Lyon packing, and Anne is left to damn the town of her birth: "Damn Lawrenceville! It was like an octopus, reaching out and trying to drag her down" (p. 243). Of course, it is Anne's mother who more accurately merits comparison to the octopus—the mother, who, in life, nearly smothers Anne within the walls of an exclusively female home and, in death, reaches out tentacles so as to imprison Anne once again. From the first pages of her novel on, Susann suggests that maternal body, maternal house, and maternal city fatally may inhibit Anne's growth.[17] With Susann, we applaud Anne's initial escape to New York City. We are glad that she runs from the mother who insists that, although daughter might add a wing to the family house once she has married, she must live in this house, a house in which only women seem to survive.[18] The maternal body, so readily associated with the stifling maternal home, becomes target; it is an easy scapegoat for all ills in the novel.

Susann encourages us to trace the unhappiness of Neely, Jen, and Anne to the body of the mother: an absent, nonnourishing mother prompts Neely into a life devoted to a self-consuming and self-destructive search for "mass love"; a mother demanding payment for past nourishment encourages Jennifer to market herself and, ultimately, the very "sign of the mother" (the breast) goes wild, proliferating and destroying; reacting against a mother's consuming imposition of self, Anne destroys her one possibility of happily married life with Lyon—and thus, like Neely and Jen, is condemned to life with the dolls.

Given that none of the "real mothers" in Susann's novel lives up to expectations for a "good-enough mother," daughters turn elsewhere, to dolls. Susann's title, of course, plays on the multiple meanings of this word: Neely, Jen, and Anne are dolls; pills are dolls; dolls, for women who remain childless, are pills. In other words, just as a little girl is surrogate mother to or finds surrogate mothers in her dolls, the three women of *Valley* discover a substitute for mother/mothering with the pills that return them to a womblike state. Describing the effect of the dolls, Susann might be describing the effect of a return to a prenatal condition. And, without exception, these descriptions are the most sensual in the novel—far more sensual than any description of lovemaking. When Jennifer, for example, takes her first pill, she reaches an all-time high; her body feels heavy with sleep, but as light as air; her mood soars as she realizes that she finally may escape waking consciousness. Obviously, Jen's bliss duplicates that of a child, pillowed within an all-provident womb environment. Susann further encourages this association as she describes the effect that two pills might have. In Jen's experience, two pills may produce "the most beautiful feeling in the world," (p. 227) a feeling of soft numbness. If mothers will not supply daughters with "soft numbness," pills will. Thus begins a most fatal pattern of compensatory consumption.

It is Jen who passes knowledge of the dolls to Neely, and then, Jen and Neely who convey this knowledge to Anne; the women join together in a consumer communication system. Given what has already been said about Neely's voracious appetite, it should come as no surprise that she indulges in such conspicuous consumption of the dolls. Having been told by Jennifer that Seconals take away your cares and supply you with nine hours of sleep a night, Neely orders them by the dozen. As chocolate marshmallow cookies and milk fail to fill the empty spaces in Neely's life, she looks to the dolls—red, yellow, and green. And, as the emptiness expands, Neely's consumption increases. In a scene that would be comic if it were not, finally, so horrific, Susann describes Neely as she takes five yellow and two red pills, slaps cream on her face, and imagines she will look "like a *living doll* when she finally got up" (p. 314; my italics). When Neely finally does get up, she is in a hospital room, victim of a nearly fatal overdose.

Anne's decision to play with the dolls occurs only very late in the novel. Her decision is motivated, however, by factors very similar to those motivating Jen and Neely. Like them, she wants to sleep, to escape from the unhappiness of her waking life into the bliss of an all-enclosed shell of somnolence: "All she wanted was a few hours of escape, a few hours to blot out this nightmare" (p. 476). Further, like Jennifer and Neely, Anne quickly steps up her pace of consumption. If one is good, what bliss might there be in two? The novel ends with Anne's decision to take double her usual dose of dolls—after all, as she notes, "it was New Year's Eve" (p. 500). In a novel that insists upon patterns of accelerated consumption and female repetition, we must read Anne's decision as a sign indicating her probable repetition of the script originally played by Jennifer and Neely, a script that ends with destruction of the leading lady.

What effect does knowledge of this fatal pattern of accelerating consumption have upon a reader? Interestingly, although we may feel sorry for this woman, surely a more general response is one of re-assurance: "yes, this is the way it is supposed to be; all women suffer emotional malnutrition; all women finally must turn to consumption for sustenance." "All": the product consumed by the reader guarantees an escape from a nightmarishly confusing "real world" landscape to a landscape of absolutes, where daughters are victims and mothers, victimizers. Anne turns to dolls for "a few hours of escape" and we turn to *Valley* for the same. Anne swallows capsules as we swallow pages. Susann suggests the analogy between character as consumer and reader as consumer when she describes the effect that Anne's first Seconal has on her. Anne takes the pills, then: "She began to read. In ten minutes the print began to blur. It was fantastic" (p. 476). Here, locating the act of reading in close proximity to that of pill-popping, Susann blurs distinctions between the two acts and between their effects; the ingestion of both pills and print leads to a comfortable, if artificial, wholeness.

Appropriately, this novel about female consumption and commodification is a commodity consumed by a female audience. Even its female author subjects herself to commodification as her portrait, on the novel's back cover, is accompanied by the blurb: "This is the doll, Jacqueline Susann, who wrote *Valley of the Dolls*. . . ." Thomas Whiteside, in a recent article documenting changes brought about by corporate and mass media marketing practices in the book publishing business, cites *Valley of the Dolls* as one of the most successful early examples of a book marketed, promoted, and distributed as a media commodity.[19] Not unlike pantyhose or laundry detergent, this commodity was touted on television and radio. Its author (and most ardent advertiser) appeared on talk shows and in shopping malls. Its sales in hardcover prompted Bantam to set a publicity director to work so as to further inflate sales in paper. The marketing paid off: *Valley* sold over 350,000 copies in hardcover and over 22 million in paper. Whiteside's analysis of the "block-buster" phenomenon in publishing is fascinating, and his location of *Valley* within this context is appropriate, but finally, Whiteside fails *Valley* as he fails to note that issues motivating his consideration of its selling—issues of changing production and consumption—motivate the book itself. Whiteside summarizes *Valley* as "a novel about three girls who separately came to New York in search of romance and success in show business and social life but, in their ambitious climb, took to pill-popping and couldn't get out of the habit."[20] Certainly, *Valley is* about three girls who came to New York, but it is also, more fundamentally, about "girls"/daughters as consumers and purveyors of an ideology of consumption.

Notes

1. In a review of Susann's *Valley of the Dolls,* Nora Ephron suggests that this escape pattern may be fundamental to women's fantasies and thus to novels that cater to these fantasies. She notes:

"Valley" had a message that had a magnetic appeal for women readers: it described the standard female fantasy—of going to the big city, striking it rich, meeting fabulous men—and went on to show every reader that she was far better off than the heroines in the book. (*New York Times Book Review* [May 11, 1969], p. 3)

Ephron's articulation of this fantasy also holds true for Kathleen Winsor's *Forever Amber* and Judith Krantz's *Scruples,* both novels in which a heroine exchanges a restricted (maternal) landscape for a city full of men.

2. Mary P. Ryan, *Womanhood in America* (New York: New Viewpoints, 1979), pp. 222-24.

3. Tom Nairn, *New Statesman* (March 8, 1968), p. 303.

4. Alice Embree, "Madison Avenue Brainwashing—The Facts," in *Sisterhood is Powerful,* ed. Robin Morgan (New York: Vintage, 1979), pp. 185-86.

5. Jacqueline Susann, *Valley of the Dolls* (New York: Bantam, 1967), p. 1. All further citations from this novel are from this edition, and page numbers will be included, in parentheses, within my text.

6. Nairn, p. 303.

7. As the stories of other female psychiatric patients corroborate, this desire to resurrect "the girl" is not restricted to girl celebrities, but applies to all girls. Mary Jane, a patient, explains that the doctors in this institution convince legal guardians to sign the patients in for longer and longer stays, promising that eventually the patients will return to society as a "bright-eyed, healthy *girls.*"

8. For documentation of the "increasing numbers of American women of all classes and races, who are seen, or who see themselves, as 'neurotic' or 'psychotic,' and who seek psychotherapeutic help and/or are psychiatrically hospitalized" see Phyllis Chesler, *Women and Madness* (New York: Avon, 1972), pp. 32-57.

9. Jennifer performs a curious inversion of the cancer patient's usual response to his/her disease. In *Illness as Metaphor,* Susan Sontag details the usual response: "In cancer, non-intelligent ('primitive,' 'embryonic,' 'atavistic') cells are multiplying and you are being replaced by the nonyou. Immunologists class the body's cancer cells as 'nonself.' " (New York: Vintage, 1978), p. 66.

10. The exception to this generalization is Tony Polar, who is the only male to talk about possible replacement. Tony is also the most "feminine" of all male characters: he functions on the level of a child, winds up in a mental institution, and suffers at the breast of maternal female figures.

11. Very early in her affair with Lyon, Anne is confronted with a similar example of "the multiplying female." Having received a telegram from her mother that necessitates a trip to Lawrenceville, Anne telephones Lyon in the middle of the night, but then finds that she cannot speak. Lyon, irate, asks if it is Elizabeth. After Anne puts down the receiver she realizes that of course there is an Elizabeth—"probably many Elizabeths" (p. 172). Replicas of Adele flourish at El Morocco, doubles of Anne arrive from employment agencies, multiples of Elizabeth cavort in Lyon's bed.

12. The nightmarish description of Anne as victim of photographers (p. 52) bears a marked resemblance to a description of Jacqueline Susann as television star: "Miss Susann's career blossomed; she was eventually stabbed, strangled, and shot on every major dramatic show on the airwaves" (in "About the Author," frontispiece to *Valley*).

13. Embree, p. 183: "Women are said to make 75 percent of all family consumption decisions. For advertisers, that is why women exist."

14. Chesler, pp. 19-20.

15. Again, the only exception to this generalized statement is Tony Polar, about whose mother we learn a considerable amount. Miriam, who plays mother to Tony after their real mother dies, blames this mother for Tony's mental illness.

16. "Female children are quite literally starved for matrimony; not for marriage, but for physical nurturance and a legacy of power and humanity from adults of their own sex ('mothers'). . . . Most women are glassed into infancy, and perhaps into some forms of madness, by an unmet need for maternal nurturance." Chesler, p. 18.

17. See, for example, Adrienne Rich's discussion of "matrophobia" in *Of Woman Born* (New York: Bantam, 1977), pp. 237-43. She notes that matrophobia can be seen "as a womanly splitting of the self, in the desire to become purged once and for all of our mother's bondage, to become individuated and free. The mother stands for the victim in ourselves, the unfree woman, the martyr" (p. 238).

18. Anne's father, for example, dies when she is twelve, leaving Anne to be brought up by mother and aunt, in grandmother's house.

19. Thomas Whiteside, "Onward and Upward with the Arts: the Blockbuster Complex," *New Yorker* (September 29, 1980), p. 72.

20. Whiteside (September 29, 1980), pp. 72, 79.

— 5 —

Scruples: "It's as Addictive as Chocolate"

Scruples is a chocolate eclair.
—Judith Krantz, *New York Times Book Review*

We created a series of important reasons centered around food to come to Macy's.
—Arthur Reiner, president of NYC Macy's

Twelve years separate the publication of Jacqueline Susann's *Valley of the Dolls* (1966) and Judith Krantz's *Scruples* (1978): twelve years of kaleidoscopic cultural change in America. For a comparative understanding of the two women's bestsellers, however, we need isolate only one aspect of this change—a transformation in the activity of shopping. No longer the simple exchange of money for goods, "New Shopping" of the 1970's becomes an act of participatory engagement, of visual and sensual play. Customers do not merely look *at* the "Disneyland-cute, adult-scale 'street of shops' at Bendel's and Macy's"; they play *in* them. Similarly, they cannot stroll passively through the chic eateries and snazzy cafés of Bloomingdale's; these environments demand an active response.[1] Within dramatically decorated arenas of "New Stores," shoppers perform and watch the performance of others; they see and are seen as they engage in acts of consumption. It is this activity that structures Krantz's bestseller; where Susann emphasizes the result of heroine Jennifer North's many shopping sprees (Jen's closets cannot contain her purchases), Krantz focuses on the spree itself, on the activity of consuming.

In writing a best-selling novel fascinated with shopping as entertainment, engagement, and engorgement, Krantz draws her audience from among those people who might enjoy filling their eyes and their stomachs in Bendel's, Bloomingdale's, or Bonwit-Teller. She feeds and further fosters appetites quickened by New Shopping as she offers her readers the same sort of visual displays and entertaining environments as the stores do. Scruples *is* a store, a store which might serve as an example of the New Shop par excellence. As we open the novel we enter "the most successful luxury shop in the world, a brilliant combination of boutique, gift shop and fashion center,"[2] and as we move from one chapter to the next we step in and out of a series of marvelous stage sets, each packed with more expensively delectable props than the one before. The women who patronize Scruples embark on a trip to Disneyland, engage in "shopping as a trip, shopping as a giggle" (p. 313); so too the women who read *Scruples;* like their sister consumers they engage in a quest for entertainment.

Just as the activity of New Shopping differs from that of shopping in the 1950's and '60's, however, the entertainment in which these readers participate differs subtly but markedly from that provided by earlier popular fiction. While we might attribute the appeal of *Gone with the Wind, Forever Amber, Peyton Place,* and *Valley of the Dolls* to their re-presentation of various interpersonal battles waged by women in the process of self-construction, such an attribution does not hold true for *Scruples.* Rather, in *Scruples* our interest is deflected first from the realm of interpersonal relationships to the realm of commodity items; "Victorian silver cookie jars, eighteenth-century beaded evening bags, French shoe buckles of rose-cut diamonds" (p. 19) not only set the scene, but steal the show. And, second, the appeal made by *Scruples* to our interest in these items does not prey upon a simple desire to acquire or collect, but on a far more primitive and powerful need to ingest and incorporate. Quite appropriately, Krantz calls her novel "a chocolate eclair" and a number of reviewers associate it with edibles of all sorts: a critic in *Cosmopolitan* claims that *Scruples* is "as addictive as chocolate"; David Brown, producer of *Jaws,* maintains that *Scruples* is "scrumptious"; and Allene Talmey, from *Vogue,* compares the plot of *Scruples* to "one of those recipes in which beef marinates for six days in thirteen curious spices."[3] Clearly, analysis of "entertainment" provided by *Scruples* may contribute to an understanding of revisions in the way all of us—but most especially women—experience ourselves in relation to each other and to the world. If, as Kennedy Fraser declares, stores "are the mirror of our time,"[4] then *Scruples* is a mirror of that mirror, reflecting at large permutations wrought during the 1970's on our fantasies, our dreams, ourselves.

Fun . . . fantasy. . . . Under Krantz's fingers, real life has a way of becoming mysterious, glamorous, legendary, sequined.[5]

A transformation of "real life" into "the sequined" might serve as plot summary for many traditional fairy tales as well as numerous paperback romances. Recognizing the apparently unending allure of the transformation plot, Judith Krantz employs it as floorplan from which to construct both her novel and the luxury emporium after which the novel is named. At the corners of her own particular adaptation of this floorplan, Krantz positions four loci of transformation: an art gallery, fun fair, theater, and restaurant. To understand the workings of Krantz's store/novel we might look first at the way each of these loci functions as a metaphor and then consider the slightly different perspective each provides on the "experience" of *Scruples*—an experience affecting both readers of the text and characters in it.

The Art Gallery

Long before Billy Ikehorn dreams of creating her own store she imbibes the skills of a merchandise collector from her French "fairy-godmother," Lilianne de Vertdulac. With this woman of "infinite sophistication" the nineteen-year-old Billy strolls along "the Rue du Faubourg-St. Honoré, analyzing and judging each object in each shopwindow as if it were one vast art gallery and they were the most discriminating of collectors" (p. 73). As Krantz compares objects in shopwindows to objects in art galleries, she elevates the former, granting shop merchandise a sanctity usually reserved for works of art. Similarly, stores which find and display this artful merchandise take on the venerable qualities of art galleries; that is, they become places of culture rather than business. In his reorganization plans for Scruples Spider Elliott specifies the necessity of such a shift. To Spider, shopping is "half like going to a good party, half like going to a friendly museum—a sensuous experience either way" (p. 314); in either case, this certainly is *not* an experience based on the exchange of cash. Krantz's frequent descriptions of the items within the Scruples's treasure chest attest to Spider's success; these descriptions read more like museum catalogs than store inventories: Chinese export armorial cachepots stand next to Waterford glass jars; tortoiseshell boxes mingle with gold-plated nutcrackers. The comparison of store to gallery, then, works to obscure the commercial base of retailing; if we think of merchandise as art we forget to look for a price tag. Further, without fear of monetary taint, we may abandon ourselves to a life spent in pursuit of things. No longer simple shoppers, we now partake of those immunity privileges granted to patrons of the arts; we are collectors, curators, "friends."[6]

The Fun Fair

While Krantz invests her store with a museum's venerability, she takes pains to avoid even a whiff of archival dowdiness; glass boxes do not imprison items from "the pillaging of Peking," nor do stern-faced guards cast looks of reproof at those patrons who cannot resist an impulse to fondle silk tapestries from the French court or authentic Ming dynasty vases. As Spider notes above, Scruples is a friendly museum, one in which patrons may play. He explains to Billy that the redecorated Scruples must function as a "playground for grown-ups" (p. 334), a place where slides and swing-sets give way to pinball machines and backgammon tables. Of most importance is the production of a fun time, the stimulation of a good mood, "whether you buy or not" (p. 316). Thus, fairgoers ("customers" does not catch the flavor here) meander through an "extraordinary, charming country store . . . bulging chockablock full of everything necessary and unnecessary" (p. 316), socialize for an hour or two in a trellised winter garden ("with its cozy discreet corners, its plumply tufted love seats, antique wicker armchairs, and round tables covered in sublimely out-of-date mauve and pink hydrangea chintz" [p. 334]), and then proceed into the main salon, Spider's amusement park, "a place to be seen, to bump into people, to be both stimulated and soothed by abundance piled on abundance" (p. 334). Obviously, the prevailing note sounded in all these "park areas" is one of abundance, plumpness, chockablock bulges. If the museum metaphor works to elevate Scruples's merchandise, the fun fair metaphor works to fill the aisles usually left empty in a gallery—not only to fill, but overfill. Piling item upon item, Krantz assures the adults-turned-children who romp through her playground that they need never experience those feelings usually associated with empty spaces: hunger, deprivation, want. Instead, they may surround themselves and be surrounded by an infinite number of fat, bulbous amusement park prizes—hanging from ceilings, projecting from walls, ascending from floors.

The Theater

Although these first two situational metaphors are of importance in setting a mood of opulence and abundance, both might be subsumed under a third more provocative, more extensive, and more characteristically Krantzian metaphor of transformational space: the store/novel as theater. This metaphor deserves considerably more attention than the previous two, both as it illustrates a substitution of surface for substance, object for subject, and as it thereby introduces processes occurring with even more insistence in the store/novel as restaurant.

In restructuring Scruples, Billy hires Ken Adams, a theatrical designer, to create a "dramatic tour de force . . . a stage set" (p. 319) on its first floor and requests decorator Billy Baldwin to transform the fitting rooms on the second into individualized set pieces (from a Moroccan seraglio to a Queen Anne boudoir in Kent). Further, to enliven these transformed spaces she employs live mannequins, bit-part actresses, to function as peripatetic hangers upon whom clothing may be draped and displayed. Thus, Scruples's patrons find themselves hemmed in by stage props and personnel, circumscribed to such an extent that they too become part of the show—and not simply as appreciative audience. Rather, as Kennedy Fraser notes in her essay on New Shopping, patrons become performers; stepping through stage sets, they step into the possibility of recasting themselves. The woman, for example, who enters Scruples discreetly clad in gray and then finds herself trying on dresses in Billy Baldwin's erotically delectable Portofino villa fitting room may never wear gray again. Certainly, this possibility of change has been employed as a commercial lure in the past. For that matter, since the 1920's a promised transformation has served as the basis for almost all advertising, especially advertising aimed at women.[7] The promise may appear explicitly in *Glamour*'s "make-over" features (let us show you "how any girl in America can be transformed through makeup, hairstyle and clothes into someone beautiful, charming and, most important, successful")[8] or implicitly in newspaper copy that encourages a woman to associate change in hairstyle or makeup with real changes in her life.[9] But both more devious and more comprehensive than these mass media ploys is that offered by Scruples to its patrons; just walk through Scruples's magic doors, onto its stage, and you will be seen differently—and hence, see yourself differently.

Krantz never spells out the dramatic details of this process; instead she relies on a series of three exemplary episodes beginning in chapter one. Each of these episodes provides a slightly different perspective on the activity of Scruples (from the vantage points of owner, arbiter of taste, and custom designer), but the transformational essence of this activity, as well as the theatrics surrounding it, remains the same in each. In the first of this chapter's episodes, an absolutely chic Billy Ikehorn Orsini drives along Rodeo Drive, "the most staggering display of luxury in the Western world," strides through the "heroically scaled double doors of Scruples" and moves into "another country . . . the most successful luxury shop in the world" (p. 11). When the Balinese doorman, dressed in black tunic and wrapped pants, opens the door of Scruples for Billy (and for us) he resembles that faithful servant in the theater, charged with dimming the house lights and raising the curtain on an entirely other world—or, in the words of Judith Krantz, "a fantasy . . . created to beguile and dazzle and tempt" (p. 11). After a few paragraphs of itemized prop description we are allowed a glimpse of the sort of magic that may occur on this stage (both of the store and of the novel) as we learn of the transformation of a "jouncingly plump teenager named Shirley Silverstein" into television superpower Maggie Mac-Gregor at age twenty-six. The transformation remains incomplete, however, until Spider adds a few finishing touches. This man puts Maggie on center stage, scrutinizes her carefully, decides which costumes complement "the real Maggie" and which must be returned to the racks. Quite simply, Spider instructs Maggie and other Scruples patrons "how to look at themselves with another pair of eyes" (p. 405). Valentine performs a very similar function for Muffie Woodstock, yet another slightly bewildered woman who comes to Scruples for help. Accustomed to life on a country estate, breeding dogs and riding horses, Muffie cannot handle the transition to life as French ambassador's wife without the aid of Valentine, who conjures up confidence for Muffie as she conjures up exactly the right costume. Muffie's sense of Val—"evidently Valentine was some sort of witch" (p. 21)—captures the essence of Valentine's skills, but Muffie's language is outdated; she more appropriately might describe both Valentine and Spider as workers in a commercial glamour factory, apprentices in the art of converting "real life" into "the sequined," wardrobe masters in a theater of transformation. Thus, the occupation of Valentine and Spider runs a close parallel to the occupation of Judith Krantz within the novel *Scruples*—that is, turning ugly ducklings into swans.

But . . . in counterfeiting reality, presenting costumed actors as, say, Restoration fops and elaborately made-up actresses as, perhaps, Victorian ladies, theater raises a number of questions about the relationship between originals and copies, between mimesis and metamorphosis. Some of the same questions arise in Judith Krantz's *Scruples*. Repeatedly, Krantz calls attention to the papier-mâché quality of many supposedly solid sets and points to duck feathers peaking out from beneath the swan's coat. She delights in descriptions of "genuine hoaxes": the restaurant constructed "exactly like an old French farmhouse built of weathered bricks and crumbling plaster, which, one was asked to believe, had been commandeered by a British flying unit during World War I" (p. 297); the Beverly Hills store "modeled exactly, meticulously and at great expense after the inside of the House of Dior in Paris," with Miss Dior perfume pervading the air (p. 274), then remodeled after Disneyland, with a few penny arcades thrown in for good measure. She enjoys explicit commentary on the role of hoax-makers: Valentine and Spider are described and describe themselves as "illusionists" (p. 285), as godparents in a Cinderella story (p. 556); Billy and Vito Orsini, store-owner and movie-producer, presented in similar fashion, engage in show-businesses which foreground the former term, background the latter (cf. pp. 318, 467). Krantz suggests that these particular hoaxes, involving the metamorphosis of one thing into another, provide harmless entertainment, permit hoax-patrons to partake of theatrical pleasures without Broadway prices. But what of those hoaxes in which the patrons themselves are transformed?

Most of the activity of *Scruples* falls into this category. Krantz presents us with poor little fat girls turned into rich, beautiful, thin women; conspicuously inelegant ladies translated into fashion paragons; inept actresses and awkward models elevated to virtuoso performers. If we compile examples of human transformation, taking care not to forget Maggie MacGregor and Muffie Woodstock cited earlier, we may trace a pattern of circumstances governing transformational magic in *Scruples*. First, this magic is practiced on women only. Vito

Orsini underlines this fact when, late in the novel, he reiterates to wife Billy, "I can't reshape myself into your idea of a convenient husband" (p. 538), dividing those who reshape themselves (women) from those who don't (men). Second, in affecting this magic, re-vision comes into play—"re-vision" not in Adrienne Rich's feminist sense of a re-looking, re-locating, and re-assessing, but rather, in a capitalist sense of reification of subject as object. For example, in chapter one, when Spider reminds Maggie that on Academy Awards night she will be beamed by satellite all over the world—"That's 300 million eyes looking at you" (p. 18)—the effect of this reminder is to lock Maggie more tightly into a perpetual self-scrutiny. Similarly, when Lilianne de Vertdulac forces Billy, who has lost some of her excess weight, to look in a mirror, Billy is confronted with a new vision of self and becomes "her own love object" (p. 67), an object meriting constant and unqualified attention. Thus, female characters participating in the magical theatrics of *Scruples* trade subjective integrity for a schizophrenic splitting of self into viewer and object viewed. The art critic John Berger articulates this process clearly as he explains that under late industrial capitalism women are split in two: "A woman must continually watch herself. She is almost continually accompanied by her own image of herself. Whilst she is walking across a room or whilst she is weeping at the death of her father, she can scarcely avoid envisaging herself walking or weeping."[10] *Scruples* intensifies this process, offering women a "new look" with each act of renewed looking, and threatening transmogrification into the old (read unloved, unbeautiful, unmagic) with each lapse of attention.

Generally, Krantz focuses on success stories: Billy becomes a "real woman" as she studies herself in the mirror; models to whom Spider makes love become "real girls" (p. 95) as they watch themselves watched by him. But this delicate collusion/collision of eyes does not always result in real girlhood. Clearly, identity construction based on visual transformation is an extremely precarious proposition; Krantz reveals just how precarious in her portrait of Melanie Adams. Melanie is the most beautiful woman Spider has ever seen: "every other girl in his life had been part of a montage of pictures flashing under the opening titles of a movie. Now the camera had finally focused on the star" (p. 109); she is a Scruples woman carried to extremes. As model, then actress, she epitomizes the "female good" within this universe; the star of Spider's imaginary movie, she attracts then focuses eyes on a self, a self perpetually changing so as to accord with those eyes. Intent upon catching a glimpse of herself in Spider's lenses, discovering herself in the response of others or merging with the image of herself she sees on screen or in photos, she relinquishes her own subjectivity; essentially, she ceases to exist.

One of the most telling examples of Melanie's "selflessness," and an example which insists on Melanie's similarity to other women in the novel, occurs when Melanie learns that her Hollywood screen tests indicate acting ability. She turns to producer Wells Cope, asks, "What now?" and agrees ecstatically when he responds: "Now I shall invent you. Isn't that what you've been waiting for?" (p. 250). Melanie's euphoria lasts throughout the filming of her first movie, during which she feels perfectly at one with the character given her to portray. When no longer in front of a camera, however, the invented Melanie collapses: "She found herself sitting in the projection room, just Melanie being— what? She began searching her eyes in the mirror again. More and more she fell into daydreams of being another" (p. 414). Having surrendered herself to Pygmalion, Galatea remains forever his slave, forever dependent on his capacity to see and mold her anew. After Cope fails her, Melanie attempts a return to Spider; she then, appropriately, disappears from the novel altogether. Interestingly, the fate of any female character in *Scruples* might follow the course charted by Melanie; all are Galateas, all human beings undergoing metamorphosis into objects. For the most part, Krantz presents these metamorphoses as desirable; everyone prefers life as a fabulously thin, marvelously chic luxury-shop owner to life as a fat, ugly Honey Hunnenwell Winthrop. But there are costs, and Melanie points to some of them.

The Restaurant

Discussion of the store/novel as theater has lead to an analysis of the sexual politics of transformation in this metaphorical context. If such transformations take their toll on the female psyche, those occurring in the store/novel as restaurant—Krantz's fourth, and controlling situational metaphor—tax this psyche beyond repair. Before examining Krantz's bill of fare for its prohibitively expensive and sexually discriminatory price schedule, however, we might consider, more generally, the ways in which Krantz constructs both Scruples the boutique and *Scruples* the novel as restaurants. She lays cornerstones for the boutique-as-restaurant in a scene between Billy, Spider, and Valentine. Billy, frantic over figures that show her magnificently conceived store to be losing money at an incredible rate, hires Valentine, a custom clothes designer, and her "partner" Spider Elliott, to save Scruples. The spunky French designer and the California-born photographer, both innocents in the retail world, fly to Beverly Hills to embark on Mission Impossible. After introductions and a morning tour of Scruples, Spider suggests lunch. When he asks about the nearest place to eat, Billy responds that the only reasonably decent place is La Bella Fontana, located across Rodeo Drive and Wilshire Boulevard, thereby necessitating two perilous crossings, several traffic island hops, and considerable energy in avoiding cars turning right-on-red. Finally seated in a curtained booth in La Fontana, Billy kicks off her shoes, Valentine rejoices in just sitting down, and Spider expounds retailing principles. He describes a typical Scruples customer who, after having spent an entire morning trying on clothes, has sore feet and an empty stomach. He points to Billy's shoes as proof and Billy angrily asks what her shoes have to do with retailing. Spider responds: "Your shoes? Nothing. Your customer's shoes? Everything. Your customer's empty stomach? Even more. It is the *key*" (p. 276; Krantz's italics). Billy then protests that she is not running a restaurant, but is trying to run a store, to which Spider retorts: "Not until you start running a restaurant" (p. 276).

With this exchange, Spider enunciates the importance of appetite in a successful sales venture. When he informs Billy that her customer's empty stomach is the key, he gives Billy her first lesson in the economics of New Shopping: stores of the late 1970's and early 1980's prosper only if they cater to the oral desires of their patrons; all cravings, whether for cashmere shawls or Kenyan coffees, must be cultivated. A woman fully aware of her own almost uncontrollable appetites, Billy can appreciate the wisdom of Spider's lesson. Thus, she not only builds a restaurant in Scruples, she also lures away one of the best chefs from Scandia to stock the restaurant's kitchen; she and the chef order smoked salmon from Scotland, caviar from Iran, crab meat from Maryland, and croissants from Paris (p. 319). If stores in the past existed to fill empty spaces by providing a setting for acquisition/incorporation (thereby functioning metaphorically as restaurants), Krantz literalizes the metaphor here as she has Billy redesign her store around a kitchen. Not surprisingly, Krantz's literalization follows a blueprint for revitalization used by many "real world" retailers during the late 1970's. At Macy's in New York City, for example, business began to improve after the opening of "The Cellar," a chic eatery. Asked to comment on the source of his store's escalating sales figures, Arthur Reiner, Macy's president, explained: "We created a series of important reasons centered around food to come to Macy's. . . . We didn't want to be just biscuits and cookies and Russell Stover candy."[11] Arthur Reiner, like Spider Elliott, is wise to the ways an empty stomach may be put to work as a goad toward further consumption.

Such is Judith Krantz's introduction of edibles into her novel. Interestingly, once in the novel-as-restaurant business, Krantz cannot seem to leave it alone, and her refusal to do so contributes to a narrative pattern that is distinctly Krantzian. In sections immediately after that depicting Valentine, Spider, and Billy at La Bella Fontana, Krantz follows these characters to other, similarly scrumptious shrines to the gods of gourmandising. Billy and Spider, for example, eat lunch under the awnings of the Santa Barbara Biltmore, "a grand, rambling old hotel . . . a mirage out of a gracious, dignified past" (p. 296). Surrounded by ,palm trees and flowers, Billy indulges in a "double sin": a club sandwich with extra mayonnaise. Valentine, not to be outdone, dines with Josh Hillman, Billy's lawyer, at the 94th Aero Squadron, that "genuine hoax" mentioned earlier and constructed, as Krantz informs us in a lengthy and closely detailed paragraph, exactly like an old French farmhouse (p. 297). Krantz does not make full use of her eye for a feast, however, until Billy meets Vito Orsini in Cannes, a location that allows Krantz to linger lovingly over accounts of late suppers at the three-star Moulin de Mougins and lunches at La Réserve, "certainly the most elegant outdoor dining room in the world" (p. 392), where Vito orders three different sauces with his crayfish, poulet à l'estragon, and a lemon soufflé. Undoubtedly the most lavishly detailed of Krantz's many consumption palaces, however, is the Boutique of La Scala Restaurant. The name of this Palace, La Boutique, conveys the crossover occurring here between restaurants as stores and stores as restaurants.[12] Krantz interrupts one of Billy's infrequent and eminently interruptable conversations with her workaholic husband Vito to sing, note by note, the praises of the Boutique. She allows herself twelve crowded sentences to substantiate her claim that "the Boutique is a way of life" (p. 430). This trattoria, boasting only seven booths and fifteen tables, is jam-packed with classy clientele and ever-so-edible items:

> The Boutique's windows, which look out on busy Beverly Drive, are filled with boxes of rare brands of pasta and bottles of imported olive oil, packages of breadsticks, jars of olives, anchovies, pimientos, and artichoke hearts. There are flasks of Chianti hanging from the ceiling, wine racks rising to meet them, and, in one corner, an open delicatessen counter." (P. 439)

These sentences should sound familiar; they bear a striking resemblance to earlier sentences describing packed interiors of Rue du Faubourg-St. Honoré shopwindows, of Scruples's fun fair department, and of its second floor seraglios and boudoirs. Here, as there, Krantz focuses on things; here, as there, this focus is at the expense of human character. Quite simply, when the Orsinis go out to dinner, their restaurant receives more sustained attention than their relationship.

While food and food establishments probably receive Krantz's most loving attention, she can be depended upon to produce purple passages whenever engaged in descriptions of consumer goods; at these times the narrative is dense and full. In contrast, narrrative sections devoted to analysis of individual characters or interaction between characters are attenuated, poverty-stricken. Certainly, an assessment of relative narrative weight is subjective and therefore problematic; but just as certainly, in comparison to *Gone with the Wind, Forever Amber, Peyton Place,* and *Valley of the Dolls, Scruples* hits both new highs (in the elevation of objects) and new lows (in the depreciation of people). Leo Bersani's discussion of variations in narrative texture may help elucidate the way in which *Scruples* differs from its foremothers. He notes that while most narratives shift back and forth between the meaningful and the meaningless,

> meaning is potentially present everywhere. What happens is that at certain moments in the story the narrative engine puffs a little more strenuously than at other moments, and the rest of the time we can, as it were, glide along on the extra steam. . . . The well-trained reader of novels knows when to look and listen with special care; certain meanings which inform the entire narrative are dramatized more starkly, or expressed more explicitly, in the privileged moments of traditional fiction.[13]

In Krantz's text, "privileged moments" belong to bottles of imported olive oil, china of the "viciously expensive Blind Earl pattern," and napkins made from "classic Provençal cotton prints from Pierre Deux on Rodeo" (p. 319). And as these objects come forward, characters recede.[14] In their recession, characters take on qualities formerly associated with background materials; they may be manipulated, arranged, and rearranged without obtruding on the more important "meaning" of Blind Earl china and Pierre Deux napkins. In other words, in Krantz's novel people are treated as objects, but objects with a small 'o', objects prior to elevation. Thus, when Krantz testifies to Spider's abilities as "arranger" by presenting us with a picture of his bookcase display of found objects—"a row of empty Dundee Orange Marmalade jars, discarded street signs, and a pair of child's ice skates, forming a group that pleased the eye in a way that could not be explained" (p. 86)—her testimony well might be read as disclosure of the way in which she operates in *Scruples,* placing one well-dressed, well-fed (but empty) character next to another, forming groups that are pleasing to the eye (if not to the mind). Earlier, it was suggested that "theatrical" transformations within the text result in a loss of female subjectivity. Prior to and round about these theatrics, however, is a text which itself has been transformed, resulting in a loss of center-stage subjectivity for both male and female characters; Vito Orsini is as much background to windows of anchovies, pimentos, and olives as Billy. A rather nice example of Krantz's decentering of the male human being in favor of the "special object" occurs early in the text, when Krantz describes young Billy's taste in men; this heroine is avid for the "jutting stiffness of an engorged prick through an expensive pair of trousers" (p. 126). Both character and narrator have no interest in any particular man, some interest in a man's engorged penis, and probably most interest in the quality of trousers covering this penis. Natalie Gittleson, writing in *The New York Times Magazine,* applauds Krantz for depicting men "as if they were sex objects, in the manner once reserved for women."[15] But actually, Krantz's novel does not effect such a reversal. Rather, as argued above, characters of both sexes suffer depreciation, minimalization, and objectification as Krantz, at the expense of character, spotlights props, settings, and "background" details.

Thus far, analysis of paragraphs devoted to the Santa Barbara Biltmore, La Réserve, and the Boutique has been employed primarily as substantiating evidence in an argument with regard to Krantz's revised valuation of character and setting, foreground and background; but these paragraphs, as well as others devoted to appetite, orality, and consumption, require analysis more specifically attentive to Krantz's manipulation of hunger. While Krantz makes reference to restaurants and various other entertainment centers (art galleries, fun fairs, and theaters) so as to further our understanding of the activity of New Shopping, her interest in this phenomenon must be read, finally, as merely one expression of a more compelling and comprehensive interest in the activity of oral consumption: feeding and eating. Certainly, Krantz writes about the transformation of a floundering department store into the world's most successful boutique; motivating this story, however, is another—the story of the transformation of a rapaciously hungry, amazingly fat little girl into a rapaciously hungry, amazingly thin young woman. It is the latter story which truly intrigues Krantz, and which she manipulates so as to intrigue her audience. Fundamentally, *Scruples* works as a novel of hunger, hunger experienced by its heroine and its readers.

At age one-and-a-half, Wilhelmina "Honey" Hunnenwell Winthrop, star of *Scruples,* loses her mother. According to Krantz, Matilda Minot Winthrop, "in a fit of absentmindedness resulting from a suspicion that she was pregnant again" (p. 40) steps into Commonwealth Avenue against the lights, is run over and killed. This unfortunate accident plays a decisive role in structuring both Krantz's novel and her heroine's life. Locating the source of mother Matilda's absentmindedness in her probable pregnancy, Krantz initiates an association of female body change with potential woe. She exploits this association throughout the novel, but most specifically with regard to her heroine. For Honey, the death of Matilda signals the onset of emotional deprivation and compensatory consumption. Deprived of maternal affection, the little girl stocks up on signs of the mother: cookies, cakes, pies with vanilla ice-cream. Of course, this stockpiling takes its toll on her body; at age ten Honey stands five feet six inches and weighs one hundred and forty-five pounds. Also at age ten Honey is required to attend Mr. de Phister's dance class, a requirement which allows Krantz to depict the "little girl," clad in a hideous blue taffeta dress, as she gratefully abandons the dance floor and heads for the refreshment table. There she gorges frantically on rich cakes, cookies, and sweet fruit punch. After "forcing the last cookies into her mouth and gulping down a

tenth cup of the grape punch" (p. 45), Honey vomits violently: "All
the cookies and all the punch disgustingly splashed across the table
of refreshments and the white linen cloth, even splattering the polished
dance floor" (p. 45). Krantz's portrait of Honey's horrible purple gush
of vomit, as well as her earlier enumeration of Honey's food intake,
verges on the prurient; with eyes (and mouth) wide open, the novelist
offers us a vision of human humiliation. Both repelled and fascinated
by the appetites of this fat female child, Krantz hastily relates a few
of Honey's high-school dietary habits, habits which bring her up to
218 pounds by graduation. It is this gothically obese creature who
travels to Paris and meets Lilianne de Vertdulac, an impoverished
French countess who takes not-so impoverished American girls into
her home for a small fee. Lilianne's first response to Honey is one
shared by many of us upon confrontation with gross physical distortion
in a member of our own sex:

her eyes widened in shocked astonishment and quick disgust as she shook
hands with Honey. Never, no never, has she seen such an immense girl. She
was a baby hippopotamus—it was incredible, a disgrace. How could this have
happened? And what would she do with her? Where would she hide her? As
she led Honey into the salon where tea was waiting, she tried to comprehend
this unexpected horror. (P. 55)

As if this response were not enough, Krantz caps off her transcription
of introductory tea-table conversation between Honey and Lilianne
with the latter's assent to the former's request that she be called "Billy"
rather than "Honey": " 'Why not?' It was certainly more appropriate,
she thought, for such fat rendered the girl almost sexless" (p. 56).

Lilianne's horrified response to the bulk of Billy is matched, however,
by Billy's horrified response to the poverty of Lilianne's dinner table.
After a repast of thin soup, soft-boiled eggs, salad, and oranges, Billy,
ferociously hungry, retreats to her room and devours a few chocolate
bars. In a sentence that reads like a bizarre parody of food fantasies
experienced by the starving Scarlett O'Hara in *Gone with the Wind,*
Krantz depicts a well-fed Billy falling asleep by meditating on second
helpings, larger portions, and "bowls and bowls of Cream of Wheat
with butter, sugar and raisins in it" (p. 60). Curiously, while Billy
complains of not receiving enough nourishment, readers of the text
receive an abundance; Krantz, as obsessed with food as her heroine,

scrupulously inventories every calorie consumed by the Vertdulac household at breakfast, lunch, and dinner (pp. 59-62). A reader, feeling comfortably full after vicariously consuming three "beautifully cooked, elegantly presented" meals, readily may share in Krantz's further abasement of her heroine; unable to control the growls of her stomach, Billy, like a petty thief, embarks on a "terrifying nightmare foray into the kitchen," tiptoeing past bedrooms and opening the garde-manger—only to find it empty. As in her attribution of Matilda's death to female hysteria, Krantz here ascribes ridiculously "uncivilized" behavior to the quirkiness of an obviously unmanageable female stomach.

Between crying herself to sleep each night and eating three thousand calories less per day, Billy loses weight. Slowly, a beautifully svelte young woman emerges from beneath layers of hippo fat. The metamorphosis is startling, so startling that it may blind us to fundamental aspects of Billy's situation and character—primarily with regard to her body and its appetites—which remain basically unchanged. First, Billy's weight loss does not effect essential change in her relationship to her own image: when fat with self-loathing, Billy develops the ability to spot "potential reflections in shopwindows blocks away" (p. 66) and avoids all confrontations with her image; when fat with self-love she continues to cultivate her ability to spot a piece of reflective glass— now, so as to grant her image the positive attention it demands. Whether retreating from or advancing toward the mirror, this woman accedes to its authority, bows to its powers, accepts its determinations. Formerly, her reflection defined her as fat, ugly; now it defines her as thin, beautiful—in both cases it objectifies her.

This objectification, clearly apparent both in other characters' response to Billy and in Billy's response to herself, is a second aspect of Billy's life which does not change following her metamorphosis. For example, upon first meeting Billy, Lilianne classifies her as a monstrosity and thereby absolves herself of personal responsibility to Billy as a human being. As Billy loses weight, Lilianne reclassifies her, puts her in a drawer marked "possibilities," and takes it upon herself to arrange Billy's life. Clearly, in her disposition toward arrangement, Lilianne continues to treat Billy as object—object which now may be put to play within a variety of interesting plots. Krantz's attribution of Lilianne's disposition to her French character ("A French woman likes possibilities almost more than perfection. They give her a chance to arrange things and arrangements, of all sorts, are a Gallic passion" [p. 64]) does nothing to mitigate Lilianne's reduction of another human being to the status of manipulatable thing. Given earlier discussion of the dangers of objectification and depersonalization inherent to various acts of transformation, we read of Lilianne's "Pygmalion impulses" (p. 66) with some skepticism. This skepticism is particularly appropriate in light of the outcome of Lilianne's scheme to marry off her newfound Cinderella to Comte Edouard de la Côte de Grace. When the latter learns that his American swan cannot produce eggs of gold, he abandons her; there is no "happily ever after" and Billy, temporarily expelled from the fairy tale plot, experiences a moment of independent subjectivity: she cries. But only a moment: very quickly Billy, like Lilianne and Edouard, begins to think of herself impersonally. She is thin; she is beautiful: "Those were the important things. The necessary things" (p. 81)—so much for subjectivity and intricacies of the individual soul.

A final "noneffect" of Billy's weight loss, similar to those articulated above as it relies on superficial revision so as to reify an already established structure, involves Billy's appetites. Although this woman successfully reduces the size of her stomach, she cannot effect a similar reduction in the dimension of her obsession. If anything, Billy is even more aware of her appetites than previously; now, however, instead of falling asleep to dreams of Cream of Wheat with butter, raisins, and sugar, she catechizes herself on her caloric intake; instead of reaching for the extra tartine at breakfast, she leaves the table only partially satisfied, having "developed an obsessive terror of ever leaving the table feeling comfortably full" (p. 67). Certainly, rituals of self control mandated by this religion of thinness appear preferable to orgies of self-indulgence but, finally, *both* are obsessive, both reflect an inordinate interest in the body. Like a victim of anorexia nervosa, Billy cuts her food intake, thereby attempting to defend herself against eating too much, but in the process of emptying her stomach, she clutters her mind; this is a woman with calorie charts branded on the brain.[16]

But not only calorie charts: while denying herself the pleasure of food consumption, Billy cannot do without consumption of some sort; she may have lost unsightly adipose tissue, but she has not lost her nearly uncontrollable appetite. Thus, she develops a strategy by which she satisfies oral cravings with nonfattening substitutes: men, clothes, and clothing stores. In chapters following Billy's metamorphosis, Krantz depicts a woman engaged in complicated conflation and substitution processes. Billy turns first to men as objects which may be devoured quickly and discarded at no cost. Following her return from Paris, Krantz's heroine spends a year in New York City, translating former food cravings into cravings for men, hundreds of men. Krantz describes Billy's sexual avidity quite simply: "As she allowed herself to feed her appetites, her appetites grew" (p. 126). The very basic connection between activities of eating and sex could not be stated more clearly.[17] Interestingly, Krantz goes even further, specifying precisely what aspects of the latter activity Billy enjoys most; she is avid for the feeling of a stiff penis, avid for the feeling of a hand on her clitoris, but *most* avid for the feeling of a penis "all the way up inside her" (p. 126). In other words, sex is a form of ingestion, incorporation—just like eating. When Billy finally settles down with Ellis Ikehorn, her first husband, she continues to feed herself sexually, while adding yet another appetitive activity to her list: Billy begins to buy things. As in her earlier consumption of men, Billy here goes to extremes, purchasing "hundreds of elegant robes to wear at dinner; dozens of pairs of beautifully tailored pants; forty tennis dresses; silk shirts by the hundreds; drawers and drawers full of handmade lingerie from Juel Park, where a pair of panties could cost $200; closets full of $2,000 dresses . . ." (p. 208). Following Ellis's stroke and the cessation of sexual activity between husband and wife, Billy comes to rely even more fully on store windows and their offerings to satisfy the desires of her voracious eyes and lush mouth. Billy knows that she purchases all these "supremely unnecessary clothes to feed, but never fill, the emptiness within," but also knows that "It's that or get fat again" (p. 208). So she wanders up Rodeo and down Camden, temporarily appeasing her hunger with the thrill of buying, acquiring. Once more, Billy's pleasure here, as in lovemaking, resides in the moment she "takes in" an object; immediately after she acquires something new "it [becomes] meaningless to her" (p. 208).

As Billy conflates sexual activity with the activities of buying and eating, the boundaries between all three enterprises blur and any one may function as substitute for any other. Given that eating poses the appalling possibility of weight gain, sex and shopping tend to be preferred; further, given that good sex is more difficult to find than a good buy, shopping usually serves as most convenient stand-in. However, as Billy realizes after a purchase or during a tabulation of her unworn wardrobe, even shopping has its limits. Having somewhat exhausted pleasures attendant upon acquisition of any individual item, Billy accedes to further escalation; her appetite now demands that she own an entire store. As she looks at a most desirable plot of land on the corner of Rodeo and Dayton, Billy is overcome with "a craving she hadn't known in years. Scruples would fill the empty spaces of her life. She wanted it. She would have it" (p. 289). Once more, Krantz's language here resembles that used earlier to describe Billy's craving for chocolate bars, eligible Jewish men, and handmade lingerie from Juel Park. Here, as there, Billy indulges her yearning, buys the land, constructs her store, and attempts to stimulate appetites of a magnitude equal to her own in other shoppers. Initially, however, Scruples fails, as Billy fails to exploit her own knowledge of female hungers as motivation for compensatory consumption. Spider Elliott, brought in to rescue Scruples from becoming a complete financial fiasco, must articulate two fundamental principles of women's retailing to Billy, principles that should be obvious from her own life. First, Scruples must fill the stomach if it is to drain the purse; and second, shópping at Scruples "should be as satisfactory as a good fuck" (p. 302). Billy, who still consumes clothes so as to avoid consuming calories, and who has "not forgotten the days when her sex life existed only in the moment of purchase" (p. 302) readily appreciates the wisdom of Spider's approach. The two of them redesign Scruples so as to further obfuscate distinctions between eating, sex and shopping, and to highlight the appeal of Scruples as a place in which one may engage (literally or vicariously) in all three. Thus, while Billy installs kitchen facilities and imports the ingredients of haute cuisine, Spider instructs Billy Baldwin to design fitting rooms that will attract women who are "gratification junkies," women who want to be stroked, women who "would like a little romance in their lives without actually deceiving their husbands" (p. 319).[18] To top this off, Spider inspects the purchases of every customer, insisting that no woman leave the store without feeling "utterly hot" for her selection, "dizzy with a desire that can't be forced any more than a faked orgasm can be enjoyed" (p. 335). With the opening of a redesigned Scruples Billy offers every woman (of adequate means, of course) the opportunity to fill life's empty spaces just as she has done.

Scruples appears to be a success: Billy revels in her solid financial investment; Billy's customers revel in their new restaurant/playground/gallery/boutique. But *Scruples* the novel does not close with the reopening of Scruples the store; chapters following the gala event document Billy's involvement with and marriage to Vito Orsini, her participation in the production of his film *Mirrors*, [19] and her reception of the news that she is pregnant. In these chapters, Krantz actually initiates a restructuring of our response to Billy's narrative as success story; final elements in the narrative suggest that the demands of Billy's stomach have not been satisfied after all, that Billy's perception/ manipulation of these demands is inadequate, incomplete, and certainly inappropriate as a model for other hungry women. Barely five months after opening the redesigned Scruples Billy realizes that "the daily details of running a store were not enough to fill her life" (p. 370). Bored and restless, Billy accepts an invitation to attend the Cannes Film Festival, where she meets Vito Orsini, a man to whom she responds immediately, a man she wants. The independent Orsini, however, is strong enough to withstand the appetitive demands of Wilhelmina Hunnenwell Winthrop Ikehorn; when they marry it is as equals, with the understanding that neither subsume/consume the other. Billy appreciates Vito's refusal to function as yet another edible object in her life, but this refusal causes problems as it brings her face to face, once more, with her own emptiness: who is Billy Ikehorn Orsini? No longer a man-eater, Billy attempts to play the role of mantender, but, given Vito's preoccupation with his career, his films, and his professional life, Billy's opportunities to tend him are minimal— too minimal to satisfy her. For example, on the evening before Academy Awards night, Billy, learning that Vito's film is to win Best Picture, dissolves into tears. Simply, she knows that the award will enable Vito to finance more deals, produce more pictures—and spend less time with her. Desolate, Billy turns to the man she loves and rarely sees: " 'The more successful you are, the less I have of you. . . . Vito, what about me? What do I do now?' " (p. 537). Her plaint is that of a child, of a "furious little girl" (p. 538). If, at age one-and-a-half, Honey Winthrop had been able to confront her mother, that befuddled pregnant lady who stepped into traffic on Commonwealth Avenue and was killed, she might have asked the same questions. But, just as Matilda Winthrop left Honey to her own devices then, so too Vito now: he reiterates his refusal to serve as raw material in Billy's construction of a "center" for herself (when Billy and Vito first meet he quite accurately describes her as "a beautiful, rich young widow who does not have a fixed center in her life" [p. 379]).

Krantz, of course, does not intend to leave her heroine in the lurch; certainly something can be found to fill the holes in this lonely little rich girl's life? Krantz allows Billy to explore various possibilities in the final pages of the novel, where the narrative slows and focuses more intently than ever before on the thoughts and emotions of various characters as they live through one day, Academy Awards day. For Billy, the day is composed of a series of personal revelations. The series begins at Scruples, where Billy tries on the skintight taffeta slip of her Awards outfit and discovers that the zipper will not close over her waist. Initially, Valentine accuses Billy of overeating, but when Billy protests that she has been too nervous to eat, Valentine whips out her tape measure, encircles Billy's waist, then her bust, and determines the real reason behind Billy's inability to wear the slip: she is pregnant. Angrily, vehemently, Billy denies Val's diagnosis, but once back at home, ensconced in her dressing room, she admits to its truth. Silently fuming at Vito ("No doubt Vito expected to turn her into an old country Italian wife, contentedly producing bambino after bambino—perhaps learning to cook with lots of olive oil and garlic—certainly getting fat" [p. 547]), Billy checks her birth control pill supply and is hit with Revelation Number Two: she has not taken a pill for three months; the responsibility for this pregnancy belongs primarily to her. At this point Billy plays amateur psychologist, asking herself "What kind of woman carefully traps herself into having a baby but doesn't want to face the fact that she is pregnant? And why?" (p. 549). Gradually Billy acknowledges that she must want a child—and probably not just one. Here then, Billy hits upon an obvious and essentially conservative answer to her earlier queries about what to do with herself and how to fill her life's empty spaces. If Krantz were writing a more socially traditional novel, Billy quite probably would embrace this answer and the novel would close with her producing one baby after the next (surely Billy would engage in this activity as obsessively, ravenously, as she formerly engaged in consumption). But, interestingly, Krantz chooses to allow her heroine an awareness of the limitations of motherhood. While enjoying a mirrored reflection of herself with one, two, and then three pillows tucked under her tunic, while acknowledging how easy it would be to slip into the joys of motherhood "under the providential cover of fruitfulness" (p. 567), Billy knows that the stuffed Memling Madonna look comes to an end after nine months and that mothers can fill themselves with and through their offspring for only so long. Billy then, accepts her pregnancy, but does not privilege it as permanent resolution of problems posed by her apparently ever-empty stomach.

Following this acceptance, in a sequence of introspective paragraphs interrupted occasionally by narrative description of the Academy Awards ceremony, Billy pursues her options yet further. Having determined that she cannot expect husband Vito or children with Vito to serve as center for her life in the future ("No, the only person with whom she would always come first, who would always belong to her, was herself" [p. 567]), she reviews various other materials with which she has attempted to construct this center in the past. Appropriately, her review is couched in the language of appetite:

Fleetingly, but implacably, Billy reminded herself of some of the things she had gobbled down in her life; once, long ago, it had been food; then, in New York, all those young men; then, after she met Ellis, the rich years of travel, too many houses, all the jewels, coming when she was so young that she was surfeited before the end of her twenties; then the clothes, the mountains of clothes, more than nine-tenths unworn; and finally, again, the men, Jake in the pool house, the others in her studio. She'd had too much, so very much too much, and so much of it unsavored, swallowed without chewing. (P. 570)

So what does this newly self-aware heroine decide to do? Actually, Billy's solution comes as no surprise (but, perhaps, as a disappointment): she will open branches of Scruples "in cities flung across continents. Rio was ripe for it—Zurich—Milan—São Paulo—Monte Carlo—all full of very rich, very bored, very elegant women" (p. 569). In other words, Billy will fill herself by feeding other hungry women; she becomes a market-mother. When Krantz relates that Billy knows "she was about to arrive at the center of her life and she didn't want to do it in a scramble of grabbing and clutching and flailing about" (p. 566) we may sympathize; but when we learn that this "center" is a chain of Scruples boutiques, we must condemn Billy's complicity in a system of consumption which preys most ferociously on female integrity and individuality.

Throughout *Scruples* Wilhelmina Hunnenwell Winthrop Ikehorn

Orsini perceives herself as a container without contents, a hollow woman. As a child, Honey recognizes that she is different from her schoolmates, all of whom "had mothers and brothers and sisters" (p. 42); as an adult she acknowledges an "emptiness within" (p. 208) and "empty spaces of her life" (p. 289). Over the years, she repeatedly attempts to discover something of substance with which to fill the void inside her. Finally, despite steps toward a self-awareness, Billy remains caught within a life-long pattern of compensatory consumption. Incapable of stepping outside this pattern so as to analyze—and thus, perhaps, resolve—needs and desires originally motivating it, Billy engages in a process of accelerated repetition, consuming more and more, and encouraging others (more specifically, other women) to lead lives of consumption. As such, Billy conspires in perpetuating an essentially inhumane and sexist market system. Preying upon emotional/physical hungers, this system promises to fill our empty stomachs and our empty lives at the same time it further sharpens our appetites and devalues our integrity as individuals. Elizabeth Fox-Genovese, in an essay on the modern American market system, finds the essence of this system in Bloomingdale's on a Saturday afternoon, in "the glitter of objects and garb, each promising to relieve the anxiety [of any individual customer] by creating a self through possession of commodities."[20] Clearly, Fox-Genovese's articulation of the role of Bloomingdale's within this system may be applied to Billy's boutique—and, more generally, to Krantz's *Scruples,* a novel so cluttered with commodities that it literally *becomes* the boutique after which it is named.

Notes

1. For more complete descriptions of this phenomenon, see Susan Porter Benson, "Palace of Consumption and Machine for Selling: The American Department Store, 1880-1940," *Radical History Review* 21 (Fall 1979), pp. 199-217; Kennedy Fraser, "On and Off the Avenue," *New Yorker* (May 11, 1981), pp. 132-35; and Jesse Kornbluth, "The Department Store as Theatre," *New York Times Magazine* (April 29, 1979), pp. 30-32, 65-66, 68, 72, 74.

2. Judith Krantz, *Scruples* (New York: Warner Books, 1978), p. 7. All further page citations from this text are from this edition and will appear in parentheses within the body of my chapter.

3. Judith Krantz, quoted by Herbert Mitgang, "Behind the Bestsellers," *New York Times Book Review* (March 19, 1978), p. 50; *Cosmopolitan* critic David

Brown quoted on inside cover of *Scruples;* Allene Talmey, *Vogue* (March 1978), p. 44.

4. Fraser, p. 135.

5. Talmey, p. 44.

6. Jesse Kornbluth is in accord with this assessment of the "artistic" potential of New Shopping. He notes that for many people, shopping in the 1980's will be "a participatory cultural experience," while adding that others may see it as "a gothic example of our society's decadence" (p. 32).

7. Stuart Ewen, in *Captains of Consciousness: Advertising and the Social Roots of the Consumer Culture* (New York: McGraw Hill, 1976), notes:

The conception of consumption as an alternative to other modes of change proliferates within business literature of the twenties. Given the recent history of anticapitalist sentiments and actions among the working class, the unpleasant possibility of "deeper changes" gave flight to a more pacified notion of social welfare that emanated from consumerization. (P. 85)

8. Kathrin Perutz, *Beyond the Lookingglass: America's Beauty Culture* (New York: Morrow, 1970), p. 14.

9. Ewen, p. 86.

10. John Berger, *Ways of Seeing* (London: Penguin, 1980), p. 46.

11. Quoted in Kornbluth, p. 65.

12. Both Jean Leon's oh-so-expensive restaurant and Billy's retailing venture are "boutiques"; the two enterprises collapse as the name of the eating establishment suggests it is a shop and the shop installs all the apparatus of an eating establishment.

13. Leo Bersani, *A Future for Astyanax: Character and Desire in Literature* (Boston: Little, Brown, 1976), p. 52.

14. John Sutherland, author of *Bestsellers: Popular Fiction of the 1970's* (London: Routledge and Kegan Paul, 1981), observes a similar object privileging in Pierre Rey's 1979 record-breaker, *The Greek:*

The world in which these super rich live is portrayed exclusively in terms of surfaces and style. Everything has a pedigree which guarantees it as out of the ordinary. . . . In this plated style everyday objects and ordinary activities . . . are always specified as special. (P. 133)

What Sutherland does not pursue is the way in which this privileging must effect an imbalance.

15. Natalie Gittelson, "Packaging of Judith Krantz," *New York Times Magazine* (March 2, 1980), p. 22.

16. See Hilde Bruche's *The Golden Cage* (Cambridge, Massachusetts: Harvard University Press, 1978), for a very clear presentation of symptoms as-

sociated with anorexia nervosa. Billy's behavior comes close to that of the typical anorexic, although Billy stops losing weight once she gets down to 127 pounds; most anorexics are not happy about the way they look until they are in the 70–80 pound category.

17. In *Fat and Thin: A Natural History of Obesity* (New York: McGraw-Hill, 1977), Anne Scott Beller quotes the results of a recent Chicago survey comparing sexual appetites of fat and thin women—results which seem to indicate that large food appetites often are associated with large sexual appetites:

a statistically overwhelming majority of the fat women stated that they would have preferred a higher coital frequency, while a significant number of the thinner subjects were perfectly contented with their sexual lots . . . these women obviously weren't overeating *instead* of having sex; their craving for both food and sex exists almost simultaneously. (P. 75)

18. Spider's description of the typical Scruples customer makes her sound very much like the customer for Harlequin romances—a woman who desires "romantic tension, domestic security and sexual excitement together in the same fantasy" (Ann Barr Snitow, "Mass Market Romance: Pornography for Women Is Different," *Radical History Review* 20 [Spring/Summer 1979], p. 158). In her essay on Harlequins and their readers Snitow asks why women *need* so much romance; we might ask the same about the women who shop at Scruples—and about the women who read *Scruples*.

19. Because of the focus of this chapter, the *Mirrors* section of *Scruples* receives scant attention. This section, however, actually requires little more than a note on the appropriateness of the title of Vito's film. Naming the production *Mirrors* Krantz suggests that chapters here reflect, in a new setting, chapters from the first half of the novel: both have to do with "show biz" as a form of entertainment, production, consumption, and objectification.

20. Elizabeth Fox-Genovese, "Yves-St. Laurent's Peasant Revolution," *Marxist Perspectives* 1 (Summer 1978), p. 71.

Conclusion

Dolly and Billy managed to have lunch together every day. Billy, who still counted, and always would, every calorie she put into her mouth, couldn't help but notice that Dolly . . . was eating a sandwich that combined slices of avocado with Russian dressing, piled on a layer of Brie, a layer of pastrami, and a layer of chopped liver, between two thick halves of a buttered, seeded roll, and on the side, potato salad with an order of extra mayonnaise.

"Damn," said Dolly. . . "we don't have time for another sandwich, do we?"

"Are you still hungry?" Billy asked in awe mingled with reproof.

—Judith Krantz, *Scruples*

She devoured every word she read and was filled with an insatiable longing for more.

—Grace Metalious, *Peyton Place*

Preceding chapters provide individual readings of five women's best-sellers. It is now time to suggest that there are patterns to be discerned in *Gone with the Wind, Forever Amber, Peyton Place, Valley of the Dolls,* and *Scruples,* patterns growing out of and speaking to specifically female fears and fantasies. What follows are a few generalizations about "the female"—as heroine, reader, and author—of five best-selling novels published in America between 1936 and 1978.

I am not the first to observe similarities in the novels under discussion here. In 1944, when Macmillan editor Harold Latham received a manuscript of quite amazing bulk from Kathleen Winsor, he immediately perceived a family likeness to the unwieldy mountain of manuscript given to him about ten years earlier by Margaret Mitchell. Upon his recommendation, Macmillan waged an aggressive advertising campaign on behalf of Winsor's novel, promoting it as "the new *Gone with the Wind.*" Macmillan's advertising paid off; while *Forever Amber* was on the bestseller charts, its sales figures rivaled those of its predecessor. Since that time, other publishing houses have employed precisely the same tactic to promote sales of their newest novels; Jacqueline Susann's *Valley of the Dolls* may be presented as a contemporary reworking of *Gone with the Wind* and Judith Krantz's *Scruples* as an even more contemporary reworking of *Valley of the Dolls.* Reviewers reinforce this networking of novels. In a *Saturday Review of Literature* essay on *Forever Amber,* for example, Paul Jordan-Smith assumes the publishing company line: "The million or so readers who have been begging for another *Gone with the Wind* now have their prayers generously answered. For in *Forever Amber* is a heroine who will remind them of Scarlett O'Hara."[1] Later reviewers are even more inclusive; an anonymous critic in the *London Sunday Telegraph* describes Jacqueline Susann's first novel, *Valley of the Dolls,* as "outdistancing *Peyton Place* and *Forever Amber,* and running neck and neck with *Gone with the Wind.*"[2] The point here is that publishers and reviewers have sold *Forever Amber, Peyton Place, Valley of the Dolls,* and *Scruples* to book buyers at least in part by convincing them that these novels run on the same track, belong to the same breed. Prior to any exploration of internal resemblances, then, we must acknowledge an imposed commercial brand: these books are written by, focused on, addressed and sold to white middle-class American women.

But aside from connections forged by a marketing establishment, do the novels evidence more intrinsic bonds? Do they form a group on the basis of anything other than sales figures? Do they, in the words of Annette Kolodny, provide evidence of another tradition, "in which women taught one another how to read and write about and out of their own unique (and sometimes isolated) contexts"?[3] The answer to these questions is yes; both explicitly and implicitly, the authors of *Gone with the Wind, Forever Amber, Peyton Place, Valley of the Dolls,* and *Scruples* engage one another in an extended conversation about the appetites of women—appetites which motivate female characters within their texts and female readers of their texts.

It may be that Jacqueline Susann in *Valley of the Dolls* and Judith Krantz in *Scruples* make explicit reference to *Gone with the Wind* so as to acknowledge their debt to the earlier novel or, perhaps, so as to substantiate promotional claims for their own inclusion within a winner's circle. In either case, the references are noteworthy. While weaving complicated webs of allusion to contemporary personalities and media stars, both Susann and Krantz steer clear of literary allusions— except to *Gone with the Wind:* it is the only novel mentioned by name in Susann's text; "Scarlett," "Rhett," and "Ashley" are among a very limited number of characters from previous fictions referred to in the text of Krantz. Susann introduces Mitchell's novel on page 24 of her own; left by herself as friend Anne Welles rushes off for a dinner date with Allen Cooper, Ethel Agnes O'Neill consumes a box of chocolate marshmallow cookies, a quart of milk, and a library copy of *Gone with the Wind.* Reaching for the book, cradling the cookies, she comments: "Wow! What an orgy!"[4] Returning several hours later to solicit Neely's advice on how to fend off Allen's repeated marriage proposals, Anne disengages Neely from this orgy only after protest: "I wouldn't leave Rhett Butler right now for anything in the world" (*VD,* p. 29). References to *Gone with the Wind* here lay the foundation for a scene occurring a few chapters later, in which Neely, confronted with a job contract, must come up with a stage name and decides upon Neely O'Hara: "It's perfect. I'm Irish, and Scarlett is my favorite person" (*VD,* p. 75). Lyon Burke proposes that Neely might find something more euphonious, but the rising star stubbornly insists that she wants to be Neely O'Hara. And so she is: daughter of both Susann and Mitchell, this character, like her namesake, lives in the shadow of an absent maternal figure, experiences intense pangs of hunger, and, finally, consumes herself in an attempt to procure "adequate" nourishment. Quite appropriately, Susann's final description of Neely, delivered by Lyon Burke, suggests that like Scarlett, Neely engages in a war for which there is no resolution—only repetition: "She'll make a comeback again—and again and again, as long as her body holds out. It's like a civil war" (*VD,* p. 498). Moreover, while Neely is associated most closely with Mitchell's heroine, Susann puts Scarlett's words in the mouths of other female characters as well; early in the novel Helen Lawson consoles herself with the line, "Well, there's always tomorrow" (*VD,* p. 85), and close to the novel's end Anne Welles employs a similar anodyne: "she was going to sleep. Tomorrow she'd think it all out" (*VD,* p. 476). Surely Susann intends us to hear the final sentence from *Gone with the Wind:* "After all, tomorrow is another day" (*GW,* p. 862).[5]

Krantz also relies on her audience's familiarity with *Gone with the Wind.* Shooting photographs for a fingernail-hardener advertisement, Spider Elliott puts an inexperienced young model at ease by comparing her favorably to Scarlett O'Hara: "you can call me Ashley or Rhett, whichever you choose, because when a girl is as beautiful as you are, she always gets her pick. Come on Scarlett, honey bun, let's try it sitting in that garden-swing—lovely!" (*Sc,* p. 101). This apparently casual reference must assume more weight when we realize that Krantz generally restricts herself to the realm of media personalities and steers clear of characters from previous fictions. A clear example of Krantz's referential preferences occurs at the end of a paragraph devoted to definitions of the terms "du chien," "chic," "elegance," and "glamour." Krantz notes: "Jacqueline Bissett and Jacqueline Onassis both have glamour, but Susan Blakely, Brenda Vacarro, Sarah Miles, and Barbara Streisand all have chien. So did Becky Sharp and Scarlett O'Hara and so did Valentine O'Neill" (*Sc,* p. 173). In the company of film and stage stars, Becky and Scarlett appear to be anomalies, but anomalies of importance; Krantz clearly intends us to chart a progression of fictional females. Further, although she makes no explicit references to Susann's females, Krantz's choice of a surname for Val (O'Neill) may be read as a suggestion that we include the feisty Ethel Agnes O'Neill of Susann's *Valley* on this chart as well. Finally, Scarlett O'Hara, Neely O'Hara, and Valentine O'Neill share more than their Irish surnames; all three suffer maternal loss.[6]

More suggestive than the explicit connections between the novels, however, are shared concerns and repeated structures. Each of these novels focuses upon a daughter's struggle in coming to terms with her mother and, concurrently, with herself as a woman and potential mother. More specifically, in depicting these struggles, the novels all rely upon the repetition and manipulation of narrative motifs and structures characteristic of a genre which feminists now identify as being particularly congenial to re-presentation of women's experience—that is, the gothic. Feminist critic Claire Kahane, for example, notes that in the forbidden center of the gothic "is the spectral presence of a dead-undead mother, archaic and all-encompassing, a ghost signifying the problematics of female identity which the heroine must confront."[7] When Kahane further specifies this center as a place "where life and death become confused, where images of birth and sexuality proliferate in complex displacements,"[8] she easily might call upon scenes from the novels of Mitchell, Winsor, Metalious, Susann, or Krantz to substantiate her observations; we find moist, dark, and deathly birthing-chambers in *Gone with the Wind* and *Forever Amber,* rotting female bodies in *Peyton Place,* cancerous breasts and gaping mouths in *Valley of the Dolls,* pregnantly fat (but ever-empty) little girls in *Scruples.* In other words, although these novels are not gothics, they partake of gothic structures and motifs as they depict heroines struggling with issues of separation, individuation, and identity construction.

Preoccupied with "definitively female conditions" of pregnancy and mother/daughter identity loss, the novels of Mitchell, Winsor, Metalious, Susann, and Krantz evidence a familial likeness to gothic fictions which speak to and of the same preoccupations. But the bestsellers also map a terrain somewhat foreign to the gothics; they encompass realms of dream as well as nightmare; their population includes romantic suitors as well as monstrous mothers. If the novels resemble each other in their management of female nightmares, does their presentation of presumably positive female fantasies provide further evidence of kinship? More specifically, do heroines of these novels draw upon a common stock of dream material? Do their authors express any sort of consensus with regard to the value of this stock—both for their heroines, and for us, their readers? A standard response to questions such as these takes note of the persistent presence within these texts of tall dark strangers—Rhett Butler, Bruce Carlton, Mike Rossi, Lyon Burke, Vito Orsini—and of heroines whose hearts seem to patter in tune: Scarlett O'Hara, Amber St. Clare, Allison MacKenzie, Anne Welles, Billy Ikehorn. These ever-so-attractive characters have been sighted in romances and novels written far earlier than those under consideration here; the bestsellers from 1936 to 1978 merely perpetuate a particular typecasting of swarthy male and fair female. One might assume that changes during these decades would provoke changes in the characters, but even a quick comparison discredits such an assumption. Mitchell, for example, describes Scarlett's first sight of Rhett: "When her eye caught his, he smiled, showing animal-white teeth below a closely clipped black mustache. He was dark of face, swarthy as a pirate. . . . There was a cool recklessness in his face and a cynical humor in his mouth" (*GW*, p. 85); ten years later Winsor describes Bruce as he is seen for the first time by Amber: "His good looks were spectacular—

but they were not the most important thing about him. For his face had an uncompromising ruthlessness and strength which marked him, in spite of his obvious aristocracy, as an adventurer and gambler, a man free from bonds and ties" (FA, p. 20). Metalious, Susann, and Krantz provide more of the same in their descriptions of female responses to Mike Rossi, Lyon Burke, and Vito Orsini, all of whom tower over all other men, blind women with flashes of their animal-white teeth and radiate recklessness, ruthlessness, and so on.[9] Are we to interpret the persistent presentation of this romantic constellation (dark male, fair female, electric love) as evidence of the ongoing and unchallenged position of romance in the fantasy life of women who read and write these texts?

When we consider the decision of these writers to include swarthy heroes and starry-eyed heroines in their fictions in conjunction with authorial commentary about women as readers, dreamers, and consumers, we may interpret this decision as a sign *not* of the stock figures' power but, rather, of an authorial reassessment. While acknowledging that involvement with a stock romantic hero serves as fantasy food for their female heroines, the novelists also expose the serious limitations of such a diet; further, as they document malnutrition suffered by female characters who confuse empty calories with real food, the novelists issue a warning to readers who may suffer under a similar confusion. Ultimately, ironically, such warnings serve to expose the superficial workings of the novels themselves; notes of caution about romance are sounded within the context of apparently romantic novels.

The two earliest of these novelists, Mitchell and Winsor, poke fewer holes in romantic balloons than do Metalious, Susann, and Krantz, but their sharp—if occasional—jabs initiate a process of progressive deflation. When Mitchell, in *Gone with the Wind,* depicts Scarlett's adolescent infatuation with Ashley Wilkes and the deplorable consequences of this infatuation, she obliges us, as readers, to reassess the assumed "innocence" of romantic visions. While Scarlett's emotions are engaged by Ashley—"a young girl's dream of the Perfect Knight"— rather than by the "dark stranger" Rhett, structural parallels between Scarlett's attachment to the former and a female reader's attachment to the latter cannot be ignored. At age fourteen Scarlett falls in love and over the years her love remains that of a fourteen-year-old: "her love was still a young girl's adoration for a man she could not understand" (GW, p. 181). More knowledgeable than Scarlett—we see, even if she doesn't, that Rhett is her appropriate match—we may criticize her adolescent naiveté. But while chiding Scarlett we run the risk of duplicating her errors; in imagining and romanticizing the possibilities of a union between Scarlett and Rhett, we rely upon Rhett to function as a repository for *our* dreams, *our* fourteen-year-old girl fantasies. The fact of the matter is, we know as little about Rhett as Scarlett knows about Ashley. Further, when Mitchell observes that Scarlett's love for Ashley is "an emotion that grew stealthily through the long days of her enforced silence, feeding on oft-thumbed memories and hopes" (*GW*, p. 182), she employs a vocabulary that implicates her readers: "oft-thumbed" generally precedes "pages" rather than "memories and hopes." The consequence of this attachment to well-worn memories may be devastating; Scarlett refuses to abandon her "storybook romance" with Ashley, thereby endangering, if not destroying, the possibility of a life with Rhett. If we take Neely O'Hara, a character in a later fiction, as an example of the typical reader of *Gone with the Wind*—"I wouldn't leave Rhett Butler now for anything in the world" (*VD*, p. 29)—we begin to see that an attachment to well-worn pages may be just as devastating.

Like Mitchell, Winsor provides us with romance at the same time that she makes fun of an overly romantic heroine. In a fashion similar to the fourteen-year-old Scarlett, Amber is swept off her feet by a stranger, a man upon whom she may project her youthful dreams and fantasies, with whom she may imagine a fulfillment of tales and stories she has heard, but never experienced. This man, Bruce Carlton, does supply Amber with a means of escape from Marygreen, but Winsor is quick to point out that Amber's life with Bruce in London is not one to be envied. With considerable sarcasm, Winsor relates Amber's thoughts as she compares Marygreen to London: formerly, Amber might spend her time

[h]elping Sarah in the still-room, spinning, dipping rushlights, cooking, setting out for the market or going to church. . . . Now she lay as long as she liked in the mornings, snuggled deep into a feather mattress, dreaming, lost in luxurious reverie. And her thoughts had just one theme: Lord Carlton. She was violently in love . . . yet she knew very little about him. (*FA*, p. 51)

Quite literally, Amber loses herself in reverie;[10] holding up her dreamy heroine for ridicule, Winsor issues a warning to her readers: take care to avoid doing the same. This warning sounds throughout the novel as Winsor never stops poking holes in Amber's illusions; in the final chapters of *Forever Amber* we must laugh as the ever-infatuated Amber prepares to hunt down her unsuspecting and happily married hero in the wilds of North America. Thus, the text partakes of both romance and mock-romance; Winsor presents the dream (Bruce is tall, dark, and handsome; Amber is beautiful, clever, and lively), then deflates it. A comment on the audience for Amber's stage performances in London might be read as evidence of Winsor's awareness of the double nature of her game:

the audience had no interest in the subtleties of character delineation. The taste was for crude gorgeous exciting effects, whether in women, scenery, or melodrama. . . . A great deal of singing and dancing, frequent changes of scenery and costume, battles and deaths and ghosts, profanity and smut and seminudity was what they liked and what they got. (*FA*, p. 180)

Like a Restoration theater manager, Winsor gives us what we like, but qualifies the gift, exposes the performance for what it is.

A much more sustained exposure occurs in Grace Metalious's *Peyton Place*. Clearly, Metalious consciously structures her text as reflection of and upon romantic formulas. If structural play were not indication enough of Metalious's duplicity as "romantic author" she also, at various times throughout her novel, allows characters to comment, implicitly or explicitly, upon the enterprise in which she is engaged. Very early in the text, we meet Allison MacKenzie, age twelve, a voracious reader of fairy tales. In documenting Allison's changing tastes for texts over the years, Metalious charts an easy progression from fairy tales to "sexy novels" and suggests that a taste for the latter may be aligned closely to a taste for the former. A comment from Allison's mother Constance also works to bridge the two genres; long after Allison has abandoned the Brothers Grimm for more contemporary accounts of love and lust, Constance continues to assume that her daughter's reading material is "innocent": "I don't have to worry about Allison. At sixteen she still loves to read fairy tales" (*PP*, p. 306). We, readers of a "sexy novel," are asked to disentangle romantic from realistic elements and to assess the "innocence" of the former. Metalious simplifies this process by providing us with several rather comic examples of characters who do not effect such a disentanglement, who confuse romantic textuality with reality. Allison and her friend Kathy, who "haunt the library, in search of books reported to be 'sexy' and . . . read them aloud to one another" (*PP,* p. 131) are most guilty of this confusion. Upon closing one of these well-thumbed library books, Kathy, for example, comments sadly: "I wish I had breasts like marble. . . . Mine have blue veins in them that show through the skin" (*PP,* p. 131). With her blue-veined breasts poor Kathy may not hope for the rewards promised to marble-breasted beauties of racy novels unless, somehow, she alters reality so as to correspond to romance (what Kathy actually does is to "draw a picture of a girl with marble breasts": a projected and perfected version of the self). Metalious, whose presentation of these readers renders them ridiculous, suggests that such a course of action is ridiculous as well.

In another one of the texts chosen by Kathy and Allison, the girls read about a hero "reduced to a perspiring jelly by the sight of his true love's breasts over the bodice of her silver lamé gown" (*PP,* p. 153) and then we read about Allison's attempts to fill out her white silk party dress so as to perform the same reduction on Rodney Harrington. Allison fails, but Helen, another Harrington girlfriend, succeeds: flirting with Rodney as he maneuvers his car out of a drive-in, Helen unbuttons her blouse and runs her hand over her breasts:

Rodney could not keep his eyes off her. She was like something that he had read about in what he termed "dirty books.". . .

"Let me," he said, reaching for her as he sped along the highway toward Concord.

She snapped her head away from him quickly. "Look out!"

It was a scream of warning, uttered too late. (P. 434)

Rodney is reduced, literally, to a "perspiring jelly" by an oncoming truck: life repeats art. Metalious accomplishes two purposes here: first, she forces readers of her book into an identification with readers *in* her book (we too select a novel reputed to be "sexy"); second, she literalizes the fantasy, disclosing its essential absurdity and potential danger. Metalious achieves a similarly double-pronged but less blatant effect when Bradley Holmes, Allison's storybook lover, reassures her about her body: " 'You are truly beautiful,' he said. 'You have the long, aristocratic legs and the exquisite breasts of a statue' " (*PP,* p. 503). "The exquisite breasts of a statue": Metalious presents Brad, and us, with a heroine right out of the sexy romance read earlier by thirteen-year-old Kathy. Our reading activity, once again, duplicates that of Metalious's characters, and as Metalious renders their activity suspect, so too ours.

While laughing at romantic pretensions and expectations, Metalious displays an awareness of her own participation in the "feed-the-fantasies" game. When her heroine Allison puts down books written by others to write a book of her own, Metalious allows Allison's authorial activity to reflect back on that of her progenitor, to expose the paradoxical nature of the enterprise in which Metalious is engaged. Stories that Allison tells to Nellie Cross betray her particular authorial orientation; all of these narratives begin in the same way: "Once upon a time . . . in a land far across the sea, there lived a beautiful princess" (*PP*, p. 132). This is, of course, the plot line Allison hopes to map out for herself, the line Metalious plays with in her novel (cf. the story of Samuel Peyton and his French-born "princess-bride" Villette). But Metalious cuts across this line with a comment from Nellie, who has seen too much of life to put her faith in such fairy-tales: "I could tell you some stories, honey, that ain't nothin' like the stories you tell me" (*PP*, p. 185). But Nellie never tells her stories; instead, Metalious tells them to us.

Later in the novel, when Allison comments upon her authorial aspirations, we may read her comments as evidence both of Metalious's own ambitions and of her deflation of these ambitions. The first such comment comes from the as-yet-unpublished writer, when she boasts of her future to friend Norman: " 'Someday,' said Allison, 'I'll write a very famous book. As famous as *Anthony Adverse,* and then I'll be a celebrity' " (*PP*, p. 269). Of course, while writing this scene, Metalious does not know of her book's future success (sales of *Peyton Place* far exceeded the landmark sales figures set by Harvey Allen's *Adverse* in 1933 and 1934);[11] she is then, precisely in Allison's position and, gently poking fun at her heroine's fantasies, Metalious smiles at her own. This smile stretches into a grin as Metalious records a later, and far more telling exchange between Allison and David Noyes. The aspiring young novelist tells a rather critically minded David that Bradley Holmes approves her conversion of the Peyton legend into a novel and that "[he] thinks it will be a big best seller" (*PP*, p. 492). Pointedly, David corrects Allison: " 'Smeller,' amended David" (*PP*, p. 492). "Smeller"? A novel about secrets at the very heart of Peyton Place?

What better description of the novel written by Metalious herself? Like Winsor, Metalious presents us with marble-legged heroines, with massively boned heroes, with all the "secrets" of romance, and then, like Winsor, she pulls back, points out the difficulty of walking with marble legs, and laughs at characters, readers, writers, who aspire to do so.

Krantz too participates in a "feed-and-tell" game—that is, she draws readers into her text by manipulating and meeting standard romantic expectations but then undercuts this process, points to its vacuity. An advertising blurb promises that reading *Scruples* will grant us, first, entrance into "the world of Scruples—the most successful luxury shop in the world, a brilliant combination of boutique, gift shop and fashion center with the world's best ready-to-wear and haute couture" (*Sc,* p. 1). Along with Billy Ikehorn, who, in the novel's first few paragraphs, strides through the heroically scaled double doors of Scruples, we readers, flipping past the cover and cover sheets of *Scruples,* seem to enter "another country, created to beguile and dazzle and tempt" (*Sc,* p. 11). As mentioned in the preceding chapter, this country provides a wide range of fantasy food, most often associated with that available in art galleries, fun fairs, theaters, and restaurants. Further, having toured the store Scruples, we partake of yet other fantasies within the novel *Scruples.* Editor Lawrence Freundlich suggests that some of these stem from Krantz's willingness to put us in the know: "Judy's writing has the same attraction as *People* magazine. You learn about the lives of men and women. She answers all the burning questions you never dared ask."[12] In other words, Krantz's novel brings us in contact not simply with romantic fictions (Scarlett, Rhett) but with fictional characters who bear a close resemblance to those real figures (anyone from *People* magazine) we romanticize.

Interestingly, while catering to our most inquisitive appetites, Krantz describes the workings of these appetites within her novel, in portraits, first, of Maggie MacGregor, a woman who reports "the inside news of show business . . . in tightly researched, completely authoritative stories, which had nothing in common with the tiny turds of coy gossip that were served up only three years ago" (*Sc,* p. 15); and second, of Maggie's incurably curious audience, every one of whom engages in "starfucking" ("a harmless way of sprinkling yourself with the glint of stardust, of gratifying, for a second, the need to feel in the know" [*Sc,* p. 347]) as they tune in to Maggie's show, purchase a movie magazine or an issue of *People.* The substitution of Judith Krantz for Maggie

MacGregor, and *Scruples*'s audience for Maggie's audience, is a simple one. Avid readers of this extended *People* magazine, we too are privy to the language of stars, to codes of correct and incorrect brand names, to secrets of the "romance industries": fashion and film. But—Krantz admits to a limitation in Maggie's performance, thereby suggesting a limitation in her own. Despite Maggie's skills as a "starfucker," despite her prolonged focus on "every pore, every eye blink, every facial line," Krantz notes that actually "this glimpse told you nothing, absolutely nothing, to explain the whys and wherefores of the mysteries of who reaches stardom and who does not" (*Sc,* p. 338). Further, as Krantz makes clear, the emptiness of the glimpse is of no importance whatsoever, "as long as the audience thought they were getting a peek at something with a grain of reality in its core, something that would allow them to feel that they 'knew' the star as a human being" (*Sc,* pp. 338-39). With this notation, Krantz points to the duplicity of her own enterprise; she, like Maggie, promises us the fullness of romantic power if we devour page after page, while acknowledging that this feast, finally, lacks real substance. Just as Mitchell's documentation of Scarlett's infatuation with Ashley serves as warning against a similar infatuation on the part of her readers, Krantz's revelation of the emptiness of Maggie's show serves as warning against a similar emptiness within Krantz's text. Once again we find ourselves in the company of a presumably romantic writer who expresses her reservations about the very process of romance.

Each of these bestsellers—*Gone with the Wind, Forever Amber, Peyton Place,* and *Scruples*—chips away at the artifice of romance; the fantasies of Scarlett, Amber, Allison, and of Maggie's audience are shown to be precisely that: fantasies. Of course, the novels will continue to be sold as works engaging standard female dream material and readers will continue to swoon over Rhett, to envy Billy. There is, however, another dream addressed in the novels, a dream which usually goes unmentioned in recitals of fantasy components, but a dream which most often is presented without qualifications: that is, to eat as much as one desires, to fill and overfill oneself, with food, affection, or pages. All of these novels pose the fantasy of an unending consumption against the fear of unappeasable hunger.

Jacqueline Susann's *Valley of the Dolls* may serve as an introductory example. In *Valley,* Susann exposes the elements of traditional romance to a much harsher light than do the other novelists. Early in this novel, when Anne Welles protests that she does not want to marry Willie Henderson because she does not love him, her mother replies: "There is no such thing as love. . . . You'll only find that kind of love in cheap movies and novels" (*VD*, p. 5); we might read Susann's novel as proof of Mrs. Welles's first statement (there is no such thing as love) and extended rebuttal of the second (*Valley is* a cheap novel, but even here the "love" that Anne Welles desires is not to be found). Susann's Prince Charmings prove to be philanderers or terminal idiots; her Cinderellas climb to the top only to tumble down into the valley. As various reviewers have observed, *Valley of the Dolls* is "a sick woman's book, a book where dream turns into nightmare."[13] These same reviewers suggest that *Valley* is a book read by women who live on the flatlands of middle-class American culture, women who may appreciate the dullness of their own lives in comparison to the chaos characteristic of the lives of Susann's heroines. While these observations contribute to an understanding of the appeal of *Valley,* it is important that we not neglect another factor of that appeal: *Valley's* presentation of female victims compensating for their victimization through consumption, frenzied consumption.

In that early sequence, mentioned previously, when Neely imbibes a quart of milk, a box of cookies, and a copy of *Gone with the Wind,* Susann not only forges a link between the activities of reading and eating, she also grants these activities an almost irresistible allure; Neely quite obviously derives a tremendous amount of sustenance from the pages of Margaret Mitchell, more sustenance than from conversations with Anne. Hungry readers of *Valley,* we may share Neely's comfortable (if illusory) sense of fullness. As the novel continues, Susann's heroines, confronted by one disappointment after another, turn away from romance of the standard variety, to a different sort of romance altogether: the swallowing of pills, pancakes, pages. Despite the compensatory nature of this consumption, Susann glories in it; as noted in a previous chapter, her description of Jennifer's pill-popping is certainly one of the most sensual to be found in the novel— far more luscious than any description of lovemaking. Susann duplicates this dreaminess in her penultimate chapter, which focuses on Anne's self-administered remedy for depression; after swallowing a few pills, a few pages of print, she is filled with "a fantastic lightness." Thus, the fantasy operating in *Valley* requires that women be emotional victims but then allows them to compensate for this victimization with orgies of appetite. Lives may be empty, but stomachs must be filled.

Stomachs do not go unnoticed in the other best-selling novels. Hunger, of course, is a driving force in the life of Scarlett O'Hara, who learns that "the stomach [has] a longer memory than the mind" and that she can "banish heartbreak but not hunger" (*GW*, p. 357).[14] Mitchell invites us to feast on Scarlett's memories of "bacon frying and rolls baking" and then, to partake in Scarlett's honeymoon extravaganza:

Best of all things in New Orleans was the food. . . . Gumboes and shrimp Creole, doves in wine and oysters in crumbly patties full of creamy sauce, mushrooms and sweetbreads and turkey livers, fish baked cunningly in oiled paper and limes. Her appetite never dulled, for whenever she remembered the everlasting goobers and dried peas and sweet potatoes at Tara, she felt an urge to gorge herself anew on Creole dishes. (*GW*, pp. 709-10)

In *Forever Amber* we come upon elaborate menus of tavern meals or dinners at Court, and in *Scruples* we scarcely can turn a page without discovering some morsels of the most delectable cuisine. While not catering to the gourmand as obsequiously as Mitchell, Winsor, and Krantz, Metalious consistently relies on the language of hunger to describe Allison's voracious appetite for reading material. How are we to account for the overwhelming hunger of these heroines? How to account for the obvious pleasure derived by both author and reader in descriptions of heroines able to eat without stinting themselves?

The novels do not offer simple answers, but rather suggest that this appetite may be the result of a combination of physical and emotional deprivations attendant upon being born female in our culture. While the cultural code does not-deny women access to physical sustenance, it demarcates certain times and places as appropriate or inappropriate for female feeding. It is, of course, obedience to this code that prompts Mammy to force-feed Scarlett prior to the Wilkes's barbeque so that Scarlett will not be guilty of displaying any sort of appetite before the assembled company. Mammy explains her policy quite clearly: "Ah has tole you an' tole you dat you kin allus tell a lady by dat she eat lak a bird. An' Ah ain' aimin' ter have you go ter Mist' Wilkes' an eat lik a fe'el han' an' gobble lak a hawg" (*GW*, p. 69). In other words, "ladies" do not eat in public; if they have stomachs, the stomachs must be filled privately, secretly. Mitchell writes of the Civil War South, but the code she depicts reappears, unchallenged, in more recent novels; not allowed to show their appetites in company, Neely and Billy compensate with binges in their bedrooms. The feeding pattern documented here bears an eerie resemblance to that characteristic of bulimi-anorexics—women who stuff themselves, then induce vomiting so that their body measurements will not bear witness to their eating binges. Discussing the pathology of this disease (one which afflicts a far greater percentage of females than males), Marilyn Lawrence notes: "It seems to be important for women not to be seen to need food in the way in which men need it. Indeed it seems that undereating is an integral part of the 'feminine' image."[15] Mammy certainly would agree.

While locating one source of female hunger in a cultural code that limits ladies to small portions, we may look to another cultural/psychological code for an understanding of emotional motivations for this hunger. This second code, which structures relations between parents and children in twentieth-century, American middle-class families, often mandates the early withdrawal of maternal affection from female children. For various reasons, mothers tend to feel more ambivalent about daughters and, thus, to withhold or temper displays of positive affection. As documented by theorists such as Phyllis Chesler (who notes that the childish orality often seen in women "is initiated by the early withdrawal or relative absence of the female and/or nurturant body from their lives")[16] and by the best-selling novelists, the emotional deprivation experienced by daughters often sets them on a life-long course of compensation. Chesler, for example, sees many women entering matrimony so as to fill the gap originally posed by maternal absence: "Female children are quite literally *starved* for matrimony: not for marriage, but for physical nurturance and a legacy of power and humanity from adults of their own sex."[17] Mitchell, Winsor, Metalious, Susann, and Krantz provide evidence of yet other courses pursued by daughters looking for maternal affection: Scarlett, in the face of all evidence to the contrary, allows herself an imaginary space (Tara) in which Mothers/Mammys may be found; Amber aligns herself with one man after another, each of whom is committed to another woman; Neely scurries for the "mass love" of an ever-more-demanding audience; Billy ingests food, men, stores, then expands the availability of these comestibles so that other women may join in her orgy. While these hungry daughters turn to various well-stocked shelves for sustenance, the female reader, also a hungry daughter (very much like Allison MacKenzie: "she devoured every word she read and was filled with an insatiable longing for more" [*PP*, p. 69]) turns to similarly well-stocked shelves of her bookstore. Having purchased a novel by Mitchell, Winsor, Metalious, Susann, or Krantz, this reader may retreat to her private reading space and indulge in a feast of pages. Under the guise of standard romance, these pages provide her with a meal guaranteed to appeal to her palate, a meal composed of dreams, nightmares, psychic and social structures affecting the lives of women—mothers and daughters—in twentieth-century American culture.

Notes

1. Paul Jordan-Smith, review of *Forever Amber*, quoted in *Saturday Review of Literature* 27, no. 43 (Oct. 21, 1944), advertisement on p. 2.

2. *London Sunday Telegraph*, quoted on inside cover of Jacqueline Susann's *Valley of the Dolls* (New York: Bantam, 1966).

3. Annette Kolodny, "A Map for Rereading." *New Literary History* 11, no. 3 (Spring 1980), p. 465.

4. Jacqueline Susann, *Valley of the Dolls* (New York: Bantam, 1966), p. 24. All further page citations from this novel, as well as from *Gone with the Wind* (New York: Pocket Books, 1965), *Forever Amber* (New York: Signet, n.d.), *Peyton Place* (New York: Dell, 1956), and *Scruples* (New York: Warner Books, 1978), are from these editions and will be included within parentheses. Page numbers will follow an abbreviation of the novel's title: *GW, FA, PP, VD,* and *Sc.*

5. Mitchell's final line may be heard in many novels of this time period. In Erica Jong's *Fear of Flying* (New York: Signet, 1973), for example, heroine Isadora Wing finds herself alone and lonely in Paris: "But where was my mother now? She hadn't saved me then and she couldn't save me now, but if only she'd appear, I'd surely be able to get through the night. Night by night, we get by. If only I could be like Scarlett O'Hara and think about it all tomorrow" (p. 280).

6. Krantz appears to have a particular affection for Mitchell's novel. In *Princess Daisy*, Krantz's second blockbuster, she also makes reference to the 1939 bestseller, and does so to intensify her presentation of a woman engaged in the rigors of giving birth to daughters.

7. Claire Kahane, "Gothic Mirrors and Feminine Identity." *Centennial Review* 24, no. 1 (Winter 1980), pp. 47-48.

8. Kahane, pp. 49-50.

9. These descriptions of Rhett and Bruce should be supplemented with

descriptions of Mike Rossi, Lyon Burke, and Vito Orsini. The first is depicted as follows:

> Michael Rossi was a handsome man, in a dark-skinned, black-haired, obviously sexual way. . . . [He] was a massively boned man with muscles that seemed to quiver every time he moved. . . . He was six feet four inches tall, weighed 212 pounds, stripped, and looked like anything but a schoolteacher. (*PP*, p. 142)

As for Lyon Burke, Susann notes that

> With all the office gossip and speculation, [Anne] was still unprepared for anyone as striking as Lyon Burke. . . . Henry Bellamy was a tall man, but Lyon Burke towered over him by a good three inches. His hair was Indian black and his skin seemed burned into a permanent tan. (*VD*, p. 15)

And, somewhat less blatantly, Krantz's Vito Orsini:

> His smile came through his eyes, not just from them, his nose had a proconsular boldness, and his coloring was bronze all over. His presence radiated a kind of flash. He had the physical authority of a great orchestra conductor. (*Sc*, p. 356)

10. Lost in her reverie, Amber bears a definite resemblance to the woman Harlequin Publishing Company imagines as its reader. As described by Tania Modleski in "The Disappearing Act: A Study of Harlequin Romances," *Signs*, 5, no. 3 (1980), Harlequin's television commercial portrays a "middle-aged woman lying on her bed holding a Harlequin novel and preparing to begin what she calls her 'disappearing act' " (p. 435).

11. Frank Luther Mott, *Golden Multitudes* (New York: Macmillan Co., 1947), p. 254.

12. Lawrence Freundlich, quoted by Natalie Gittelson, "Packaging of Judith Krantz," *New York Times Magazine* (March 2, 1980), p. 23.

13. Tom Nairn, "Sex and Death," *New Statesman* (March 8, 1968), p. 303; see also Sara Davidson, *Harper's* 239 (October 1969), pp. 65-71.

14. While banishing *Gone with the Wind* from his bookshelves as a "bad novel," "a novel false to the human heart," Floyd Watkins—quite unintentionally I am sure—hits upon one of *Gone with the Wind*'s strengths when he notes that it "creates a myth which seems to ease the *hunger* of all extravagantly Southern and little romantic souls" ("*Gone with the Wind* as Vulgar Literature." *Southern Literary Journal* 2 [Spring 1970], p. 89; my italics).

15. Marilyn Lawrence, "Anorexia Nervosa—The Control Paradox." *Women's Studies International Quarterly*, 2 (1979), p. 97.

16. Phyllis Chesler, *Women and Madness* (New York: Avon, 1972), pp. 19-20.

17. Chesler, p. 18; my italics.

Bibliography

Adams, Donald. "A Fine Novel of the Civil War." *New York Times Book Review* (July 5, 1936), 1.

Asheim, Lester. "Portraits of the Book Reader as Depicted in Current Research." In *Mass Communications,* ed. Wilbur Schramm. Urbana: University of Illinois Press, 1949, pp. 424-29.

Atwood, Margaret. *Life Before Man.* New York: Simon and Schuster, 1979.

Austen, James C. and Koch, Donald (eds.). *Popular Literature in America: A Symposium in Honor of Lyon H. Richardson.* Bowling Green, Ohio: Bowling Green Popular Press, 1972.

Baldwin, Faith. "The Woman Who Wrote *Gone with the Wind.*" *Pictorial Review,* 28 (Mar. 1937), 4, 69-70, 72.

Banning, Margaret Culkin. "Who Escapes?" *Saturday Review of Literature* 16 (July 17, 1937), 3-4, 14-15.

Baym, Nina. *Women's Fiction: A Guide to Novels by and about Women in America, 1820-1870.* Ithaca: Cornell University Press, 1978.

Beard, Mary. *America through Women's Eyes.* New York: Macmillan, 1933.

Bell, Quentin. *On Human Finery.* New York: A. A. Wyn, Inc., 1949.

Beller, Anne Scott. *Fat and Thin: A Natural History of Obesity.* New York: McGraw-Hill, 1977.

Benét, Stephen Vincent. "Georgia Marches Through." *Saturday Review of Literature* 14 (July 4, 1936), 5.

Benson, Susan Porter. "Palace of Consumption and Machine for Selling: The American Department Store, 1880-1940." *Radical History Review* 21 (Fall 1979), 199-217.

Berger, John. *Ways of Seeing.* London: Penguin Books, 1980.

Berke, Jacqueline. " 'Mother, I can do it myself!' The Self-sufficient Heroine in Popular Girls' Fiction." *Women's Studies* 6 (1979), 187-203.

Bersani, Leo. *A Future for Astyanax: Character and Desire in Literature.* Boston: Little, Brown and Co., 1976.

Bettelheim, Bruno. *The Uses of Enchantment.* New York: Alfred A. Knopf, 1977.

Binsse, Henry Lorin. Untitled review of *Forever Amber. Commonweal* 41 (Dec. 29, 1944), 282.

Bishop, John Peale. "War and No Peace." *New Republic* 87 (July 15, 1936), 301.

Bocca, Geoffrey. *Best Seller: A Nostalgic Celebration of the Less-Than-Great Books You Have Always Been Afraid to Admit You Loved.* New York: Wyndham Books, 1981.

Bode, Carl. *The Half-World of American Culture: A Miscellany.* Carbondale, Illinois: Southern Illinois University Press, 1965.

Britton, Anne, and Collin, Marion. *Romantic Fiction.* London: T. V. Boardman, 1960.

Bruche, Hilde. *The Golden Cage: The Enigma of Anorexia Nervosa.* Cambridge, Massachusetts: Harvard University Press, 1978.

Cantor, Norman, and Wertham, Michael, eds. *History of Popular Culture.* New York: Macmillan, 1968.

Cappon, Daniel. *Eating, Loving and Dying: A Psychology of Appetites.* Toronto: University of Toronto Press, 1973.

Cawelti, John. *Adventure, Mystery and Romance.* Chicago: University of Chicago Press, 1976.

———. *The Six-Gun Mystique.* Bowling Green, Ohio: Bowling Green University Popular Press, 1971.

Cerf, Bennett. "The Life of Rally." *Saturday Review of Literature* 29 (Jan. 5, 1946), 20-22.

———. "Trade Winds." *Saturday Review of Literature* 27 (Nov. 4, 1944), 18.

Chabot, C. Barry. "Reading Readers Reading Readers Reading." *Diacritics* 5 (Fall 1975), 24-31.

Chamber, A., and Kalter, S. "Pages." *People* 12 (Oct. 1, 1979), 77-78.

Chase, Richard. *The American Novel and Its Tradition.* Garden City, New York: Doubleday, 1957.

Chernin, Kim. "How Women's Diets Reflect Fear of Power." *New York Times Magazine* (Oct. 11, 1981), 38-50.

Chesler, Phyllis. *Women and Madness.* New York: Avon, 1972.

Chodorow, Nancy. "Family Structure and Feminine Personality." In *Women, Culture and Society,* ed. M. Rosaldo and L. Lamphere. Stanford: Stanford University Press, 1974.

———. *The Reproduction of Mothering.* Berkeley: University of California Press, 1978.

Cockburn, Claud. *Bestseller: The Books That Everyone Read, 1900 to 1939.* London: Sidgwick and Jackson, 1972.

Coffin, P. "Kay Winsor Launches a New Career." *Look* 18 (Aug. 10, 1954), 70.

Cordell, A. "Strange Story behind *Gone with the Wind.*" *Coronet* 49 (Feb. 1961), 98-104.

Cowart, David. "Oedipal Dynamics in *Jane Eyre.*" *Literature and Psychology* 31 (1981), 33-37.

Cowley, Malcolm. "Classics and Best-Sellers." *New Republic* (Dec. 22, 1947), 25-27.

——. Untitled review of *Gone with the Wind. New Republic* (Sept. 16, 1936), 161.

Daniel, Frank. "Cinderella City: Atlanta Sees *Gone with the Wind.*" *Saturday Review of Literature* 21 (Dec. 23, 1936), 10-12.

Davidson, Cathy, and Broner, E. M. (eds.). *The Lost Tradition: Mothers and Daughters in Literature.* New York: F. Ungar, 1980.

Davidson, Sara. "Jacqueline Susann: The Writing Machine." *Harper's* (Oct. 1969), 65-71.

Dawson, Gaillard. "*Gone with the Wind* as Bildungsroman." *Georgia Review* 28 (Spring 1974), 9-18.

Day, Doris. "Doris Day Remembers: My Friend Jackie." *Ladies' Home Journal* (Jan. 1975), 58.

Deutsch, Helene. *Selected Problems of Adolescence.* New York: International Universities Press, 1967.

Diehl, Joanne Feit. " 'Come Slowly-Eden': An Exploration of Women Poets and Their Muse." *Signs* 3 (1978), 572-87.

Douglas, Ann. *The Feminization of American Culture.* New York: Avon, 1978.

——. "Soft-Porn Culture." *New Republic* (Aug. 30, 1980), 25-29.

Drake, Robert Y., Jr. "Tara Twenty Years After." *Georgia Review* 12 (Summer 1958), 142-49.

Du Bois, William. "Jumbo Romance of Restoration London." *New York Times Book Review* (Oct. 15, 1944), 7.

Easton, Barbara. "Feminism and the Contemporary Family." *Socialist Review* (May-June 1978), 30.

Edwards, Augusta D. "My Most Unforgettable Character." *Reader's Digest* (Mar. 1962), 117-21.

Embree, Alice. "Madison Avenue Brainwashing—The Facts." In *Sisterhood is Powerful,* ed. Robin Morgan. New York: Vintage, 1970.

Ephron, Nora. "The Love Machine." *New York Times Book Review* (May 11, 1969), 3.

——. *Wallflower at the Orgy.* New York: Bantam, 1980.

Ettorre, Barbara. "Stores Try Theatrical Selling Techniques." *New York Times* (Jan. 23, 1979), D1, D4.

Ewen, Stuart. *Captains of Consciousness: Advertising and the Social Roots of the Consumer Culture.* New York: McGraw Hill, 1976.

Faderman, Lillian, and Bernikow, Louise. "Comments." *Signs* 4 (1978), 188-91, 191-95.

Farr, Finis. *Margaret Mitchell of Atlanta.* New York: Morrow, 1965.

Fiedler, Leslie. *The Inadvertent Epic.* New York: Simon and Schuster, 1979.

————. *Love and Death in the American Novel.* New York: Stein and Day, 1966.

Fox-Genovese, Elizabeth. "The New Female Literary Culture." *Antioch Review* 38 (Spring 1980), 193-217.

————. "Yves Saint Laurent's Peasant Revolution." *Marxist Perspectives* 1 (Summer 1978), 58-92.

Fraser, Kennedy. "Feminine Fashions." *New Yorker* (Aug. 10, 1981), 86-88.

————. "On and Off the Avenue." *New Yorker* (May 11, 1981), 126-35.

Freud, Sigmund. "Analysis Terminable and Interminable," *The Standard Edition of the Complete Psychological Works of Sigmund Freud,* vol. 23, trans. and ed., James Strachey. London: Hogarth Press, 1953.

Friedrich, Otto. "Farewell to Peyton Place." *Esquire* (Dec. 1971), 160-68.

Furman, Nelly. "The Study of Women and Language: Comment on Vol. 3, no. 3." *Signs* 4, no. 1 (Autumn 1978), 183-85.

Gardiner, Judith Kegan. "On Female Identity and Writing by Women." In *Writing and Sexual Difference,* ed. Elizabeth Abel. Chicago: University of Chicago Press, 1982.

Geary, Susan. "The Domestic Novel as a Commercial Commodity: Making a Bestseller in the 1850's." *Bibliographic Society of America Papers* 70 (July 1976), 365-93.

Gelfant, Blanche. "Sister to Faust: The City's 'Hungry Woman' as Heroine." *Novel* (Fall 1981), 23-38.

Gilbert, Douglas. "Amours of Charles II Ruled Out as Film Fare." *New York World Telegram* (Oct. 11, 1944), 1.

Gilbert, Sandra M., and Gubar, Susan. *The Madwoman in the Attic.* New Haven: Yale University Press, 1979.

Gittleson, N. "Packaging of Judith Krantz." *New York Times Magazine* (March 2, 1980), 22-24.

Gordon, Michael (ed.). *The American Family in Social-Historical Perspective.* New York: St. Martin's Press, 1973.

Granberry, Edwin. "The Private Life of Margaret Mitchell." *Collier's* 99 (Mar. 1937), 22, 24, 26.

Greene, Suzanne Ellery. *Books for Pleasure: Popular Fiction, 1914-45.* Bowling Green, Ohio: Bowling Green Popular Press, 1974.

Grover, Robert L. "Margaret Mitchell, the Lady from Atlanta." *Georgia Historical Quarterly* 52 (March 1968), 53-69.

Gutwilling, Robert. "In History There's Never Been Anything Like It." *New York Times Book Review* (June 25, 1961), 6.

Hackett, Alice Payne, and Burke, James Henry. *Eighty Years of Best Sellers, 1895-1975.* New York: R. R. Bowker Co., 1977.

Hart, James D. *The Popular Book: A History of America's Literary Taste.* Berkeley: University of California Press, 1961.

Harvey, John Frederick. *"The Content Characteristics of Best-selling Novels."* Ph.D. Diss., University of Chicago, 1949.

Harwell, Richard (ed.). *Margaret Mitchell's 'Gone with the Wind' Letters: 1936-46.* New York: Macmillan Co., 1976.

Hinding, Andrea, ed. *Women's History Sources: A Guide to Archives and Manuscript Collections in the United States.* New York: R. R. Bowker, 1979.

Hogan, Phyllis. Untitled review of *Peyton Place. San Francisco Chronicle* (Sept. 28, 1956), 17.

Hoggart, Richard. *The Uses of Literacy.* Fair Lawn, New Jersey: Essential Books, 1957.

Holland, Norman N. *The Dynamics of Literary Response.* New York: Norton, 1975.

Howard, J. "Happiness is Being Number One." *Life* (Aug. 19, 1966), 68-75.

Howden-Smith, Arthur D. "Kathleen Winsor's Salty Dish," *Saturday Review of Literature* 47 (Oct. 14, 1944), 44.

Inge, Thomas (ed.). *Handbook of American Popular Culture.* Westport, Connecticut: Greenwood Press, 1980.

Jacobs, Su-Ellen. *Women in Perspective.* Urbana, Illinois: University of Illinois Press, 1974.

Jehlen, Myra. "Archimedes and the Paradox of Feminist Criticism." *Signs* 6 (Summer 1981), 575-601.

Jones, Anne Goodwyn. *Tomorrow Is Another Day.* Baton Rouge: Louisiana State University Press, 1981.

Jones, Marian Elder. "Me and My Book." *Georgia Review* 16 (Summer 1962), 180-86.

Jong, Erica. *Fear of Flying.* New York: Signet, 1973.

Kahane, Clare. "Gothic Mirrors and Feminine Identity." *Centennial Review* 24, no. 1 (Winter 1980), 43-64.

Knebel, Fletcher. "Scarlett O'Hara's Millions." *Look* (Dec. 3, 1963), 39-42.

Kolodny, Annette. "A Map for Rereading: Or, Gender and the Interpretation of Literary Texts." *New Literary History* 11 (Spring 1980), 451-67.

Kornbluth, Jesse. "The Department Store as Theatre." *New York Times Magazine* (April 29, 1979), 30-32, 65-66, 68, 72, 74.

Krantz, Judith. "A Few Words to a Beginning Writer." *Writer* 93 (Dec. 1980), 18-19.

———. *Princess Daisy.* New York: Crown, 1980.

———. *Scruples.* New York: Warner Books, 1978.

Krier, Beth Ann. "The Midas Touch of the Bestselling Krantzes." *Los Angeles Times* (Sept. 25, 1979), 6.

Kunzle, David. "Dress Reform as Anti-Feminism." *Signs* 2 (1977), 570-79.

Latham, Harold S. *My Life in Publishing.* New York: Dutton, 1965.

Lawrence, Marilyn. "Anorexia Nervosa—The Control Paradox." *Women's Studies International Quarterly* 2 (1979), 93-101.

Legman, G. *Love and Death.* New York: Breaking Point, 1949.

Lerner, Gerda. "The Lady and the Mill Girl: Change in the Status of Women in the Age of Jackson." *Midcontinent American Studies Journal* 10 (Spring 1969), 5-15.

Levin, Martin. "Reader's Report." *New York Times Book Review* 71 (April 10, 1966), 30.

Lieberman, Marcia R. " 'Some Day My Prince Will Come': Female Acculturation through the Fairy Tale." *College English* 34 (Dec. 1972), 383-95.

Link, Henry C., and Hopf, Harry. *People and Books: A Study of Reading and Book-Buying Habits.* New York: Book Industry Committee, 1946.

Locher, Frances (ed.). "Kathleen Winsor." In *Contemporary Authors* vols. 97-100. Detroit: Gale Research Co., 1981.

Luedtke, Luther S., ed. *The Study of American Culture/Contemporary Conflicts.* Deland, Florida: Everett/Edwards, Inc., 1977.

Lytle, Andrew Nelson. "The Image as Guide to Meaning in the Historical Novel." *Sewanee Review* 61 (1953), 410-21.

Macfarlane, Alan. *The Family Life of Ralph Josselin: An Essay in Historical Anthropology.* Cambridge, England: Cambridge University Press, 1978.

McGill, Ralph. "*Gone with the Wind,* the Story behind the Story." *Red Barrel* 15 (Sept. 1936), 14-20.

McNeal, James U. *Dimensions of Consumer Behavior.* New York: Appleton-Century-Crofts, 1969.

Malin, Irving. *The New American Gothic.* Carbondale, Illinois: Southern Illinois University Press, 1962.

Martynova, A. "Daisy Syndrome." *World Press Review* 27 (Nov. 1980), 52.

Mealand, Richard. "Books into Film." *Publisher's Weekly* 146 (Sept. 16, 1944), 999.

Metalious, Grace. *Peyton Place.* New York: Dell, 1956.

———. *Return to Peyton Place.* New York: Dell, 1959.

Miller, William. *The Book Industry.* New York: Columbia University Press, 1949.

Millum, Trevor. *Images of Women: Advertising in Women's Magazines.* Totowa, New Jersey: Rowman and Littlefield, 1975.

Mitchell, Margaret. *Gone with the Wind.* New York: Macmillan, 1936.

Mitgang, Herbert. "Behind the Bestsellers." *New York Times Book Review* (Mar. 19, 1978), 50.

Mizejewski, Linda. "Scarlett O'Hara and Reform Feminism." Unpublished paper, read at Popular Culture Convention in Cincinnati, Ohio, 1981.

Modleski, Tania. "The Disappearing Act: A Study of Harlequin Romances." *Signs* 5, no. 3 (1980), 435-48.

————. "The Search for Tomorrow in Today's Soap Operas." *Film Quarterly* 33 (Fall 1979), 12-21.

Moers, Ellen. *Literary Women.* Garden City, New York: Doubleday, 1976.

Morton, Marion J. " 'My Dear, I Don't Give a Damn': Scarlett O'Hara and the Great Depression." *Frontiers* 5, no. 3 (1981), 53-56.

Mott, Frank Luther. *Golden Multitudes: The Story of Best Sellers.* New York: Macmillan, 1947.

Mulvey, Laura. "Visual Pleasure and the Narrative Cinema." *Screen* 16 (Autumn 1975), 6-18.

Murstein, Bernard. *Love, Sex and Marriage through the Ages.* New York: Springer, 1974.

Naether, Carl A. *Advertising to Women.* New York: Harper and Row, 1928.

Nairn, Tom. "Sex and Death." *New Statesman* (Mar. 8, 1968), 303.

Nugent, F. S. *"Forever Amber* or Crime Doesn't Pay; Hollywood Version." *New York Times Magazine* (Aug. 4, 1946), 12.

Nye, Russell. *The Unembarrassed Muse: The Popular Arts in America.* New York: Dial, 1970.

Ohmann, Carol. "Emily Bronte in the Hands of Male Critics," *College English* 32 (May 1971), 906-13.

Perutz, Kathrin. *Beyond the Lookingglass: America's Beauty Culture.* New York: Morrow, 1970.

Propp, V. *Morphology of the Folktale.* Austin: University of Texas, 1977.

Purdy, Ken. "Valley of the Dollars." *Saturday Evening Post* (Feb. 24, 1968), 76-78.

Reed, Rex. "Remembering Jacqueline Susann." *Ladies' Home Journal* (Jan. 1975), 52-58.

Reilly, S. "Out of the Pages." *People* 9 (June 26, 1978), 56-57.

Rich, Adrienne. *Of Woman Born.* New York: Bantam, 1977.

Rich, Stuart U. *Shopping Behavior of Department Store Customers.* Cambridge, Massachusetts: Harvard University Press, 1963.

Rosenbaum, Belle. "Why Do They Read It?" *Scribner's* 102 (Aug. 1937), 69.

Rosenberg, Bernard, and White, David Manning, (eds.). *Mass Culture: The Popular Arts in America.* Glencoe, Illinois: Free Press, 1957.

Rowe, Karen E. "Feminism and Fairy Tales." *Women's Studies* 6 (1969), 237-57.

Russ, Joanna. "The Modern Gothic." *Journal of Popular Culture* 6 (Spring 1973), 666-91.

Ryan, Mary P. *Womanhood in America: From Colonial Times to the Present.* New York: New Viewpoints, 1979.

Slater, Philip E. *The Pursuit of Loneliness.* Boston: Beacon, 1970.

Smith, Henry Nash. *Democracy and the Novel.* New York: Oxford, 1978.

Smith, Roger H. (ed.). *The American Reading Public.* New York: R. R. Bowker, 1964.

Snitow, Ann Barr. "Mass Market Pornography: Pornography for Women Is Different." *Radical History Review* 20 (Spring/Summer 1979), 141-61.

Sontag, Susan. *Illness as Metaphor.* New York: Vintage, 1978.

Steinem, Gloria. Untitled review of *Valley of the Dolls. Book Week* 24 (April 1966), 11.

Stern, Jerome. "*Gone with the Wind:* The South as America." *Southern Humanities Review* 6 (1972), 5-12.

Stone, Kay. "Things Walt Disney Never Told Us." *Journal of American Folklore* 88 (1975), 42-49.

Street, James H. "*Gone with the Wind:* A Woman's Way of Telling the South's True Story." *New York World Telegram* (Oct. 3, 1936), 8, 9, 12.

Stuckey, W. J. *The Pulitzer Prize Novel: A Critical Backward Look.* Norman, Oklahoma: University of Oklahoma Press, 1966.

Sugar, Max (ed.). *Female Adolescent Development.* New York: Brunner/Mazel, 1979.

Susann, Jacqueline. *Valley of the Dolls.* New York: Bantam, 1967.

Susman, Warren (ed.). *Culture and Commitment: 1929-1945.* New York: Braziller, 1973.

Sutherland, John. *Bestsellers: Popular Fiction of the 1970's.* London: Routledge and Kegan Paul, 1981.

Talmey, Allene. Untitled review of *Scruples. Vogue* (March 1978), 44.

Toth, Emily. *Inside Peyton Place.* Garden City, New Jersey: Doubleday and Co., 1981.

Uzzell, Thomas H. "Love Pulps." *Scribner's* 103 (April 1938), 36-41.

———. "Mob Reading: Romantic Ingredients in the Super Best Sellers," *Saturday Review of Literature* 17 (Nov. 29, 1937), 3-4, 16, 18.

Watkins, Floyd C. "*Gone with the Wind* as Vulgar Literature." *Southern Literary Journal* 2 (Spring 1970), 86-103.

Welter, Barbara. "The Cult of True Womanhood, 1820-1860." *American Quarterly* 18 (Summer 1966), 151-57.

Van Auken, Sheldon. "The Southern Historical Novel in the Early Twentieth-Century." *Journal of Southern History* 14 (May 1948), 157-91.

Veblen, Thorstein. *Theory of the Leisure Class.* New York: Modern Library, 1961.

Webb, Kay (ed.). *Grimm's Fairy Tales.* Harmondsworth, England: Penguin, 1974.

Weibel, Kathryn. *Mirror Mirror: Images of Women Reflected in Popular Culture.* Garden City, New York: Doubleday, Anchor Books, 1977.

Whiteside, Thomas. "Onward and Upward with the Arts: The Blockbuster

Complex." *New Yorker* (Sept. 29, 1981, pp. 48-101; Oct. 6, 1981, pp. 63-146; Oct. 13, 1981, pp. 52-143).

Winsor, Kathleen. *Forever Amber.* New York: Macmillan, 1944.

Woodward, Helen. *The Lady Persuaders.* New York: Harcourt, Brace and Co., 1960.

Young, Stark. "More Encaustics for Southerners." *Virginia Quarterly Review* 13 (1937), 35-48.

Index

About the Author

MADONNE M. MINER is Assistant Professor of English at the University of Wyoming. Her article " 'Neither Mother, Wife, Nor England's Queen': The Roles of Women in Richard III" has appeared in *The Woman's Part,* and "Hints That Veil" has appeared in *The Markham Review.*